ENDORSEMEN

I love it when someone can take biblical truth and apply it to life experiences. Pastor Phil Hopper does a thorough exegesis of Ephesians 6, teaching us how to win the war over our enemy. Piece by piece and truth upon truth you can learn to win.

DR. JOHNNY M. HUNT
Senior Pastor, First Baptist Church Woodstock
Senior Vice President, Evangelism and Leadership for the North
American Mission Board

Pastor Phil has written the most practical book on spiritual warfare that I have read. Reflecting on his experience in physical warfare as a Kansas City Police Department officer and his time as a pastor experiencing every trick and lie of the enemy, Pastor Phil gives a very straightforward guide to understanding and applying the principles of war with the weapons of war as outlined in Scripture. Every Christian needs to have a copy of this book. I loved it.

WILLIAM G. (JERRY) BOYKIN, LTG
Retired, U.S. Army
Executive Vice President, Family Research Council

Victory in the Christian life is more talked about than lived. Satan is our real enemy, not people, situations, and circumstances. Phil Hopper ignites the vision and shares the path to walking in spiritual victory in this newest book, *The Weapons of Our Warfare*. Victory is possible!

DR. RONNIE FLOYD
President-CEO, Southern Baptist
Convention Executive Committee

The Weapons of Our Warfare by Pastor Phil is, quite simply, a MUST READ! The way the book blends real-world events with the spiritual battle with which we all struggle creates a tactical map for us to win. The book can't be described—it has to be experienced. Break open the cover, start reading, experience it—and there are things in your spiritual world you will never approach the same way again!

ROBERT J. KUEHL
Deputy Chief, Metropolitan Police Department

Each and every Christian needs to understand that we have an enemy who wants to obliterate us. *The Weapons of Our Warfare* is a great read about putting on the armor of God and fighting from our position of victory poured out on the cross by our Lord and Savior, Jesus Christ.

JOBY MARTIN
Lead Pastor, Church of Eleven22

In his first book, *Defeating the Enemy,* Phil Hopper showed us how Satan works behind the scenes, bent on destroying lives. In *The Weapons of our Warfare,* he helps us discover the weapons God provides us to battle this ever-present, unrelenting evil. Armed with the truth of the Bible, his real-life SWAT experiences and easy-to-read writing style, Hopper has again encouraged me to not only recognize the war that continually rages against us, but to arm, engage, and fight the enemy!

LES NORMAN
Former KC Royal and Syndicated Radio Host

THE
WEAPONS
— OF OUR —
WARFARE

DESTINY IMAGE BOOKS BY PHIL HOPPER

Defeating the Enemy

THE
WEAPONS
— OF OUR —
WARFARE

USING THE FULL ARMOR OF GOD TO DEFEAT THE ENEMY

PHIL HOPPER

DESTINY IMAGE® PUBLISHERS, INC.

P.O. Box 310, Shippensburg, PA 17257-0310

"Promoting Inspired Lives."

This book and all other Destiny Image and Destiny Image Fiction books are available at Christian bookstores and distributors worldwide.

Cover design by Eileen Rockwell

Interior design by Terry Clifton

For more information on foreign distributors, call 717-532-3040.

Reach us on the Internet: www.destinyimage.com.

ISBN 13 TP: 978-0-7684-5242-6

ISBN 13 eBook: 978-0-7684-5243-3

ISBN 13 HC: 978-0-7684-5245-7

ISBN 13 LP: 978-0-7684-5244-0

For Worldwide Distribution, Printed in the U.S.A.

1 2 3 4 5 6 7 8 / 24 23 22 21 20

DEDICATION

I dedicate this book to the congregation and Kingdom Warriors of Abundant Life. You are a beautiful bride and body of our Lord Jesus Christ. And it's my overwhelming honor to be your pastor. I love you very much.

ACKNOWLEDGMENTS

Nothing of significance is ever accomplished alone. I acknowledge my Executive Assistant, Lisa Deacy, for the many hours she personally invested behind the scenes to produce this book. Lisa, thank you for your labor for Jesus. I also acknowledge our amazing staff of men and women at Abundant Life. Thank you for your dedication. I acknowledge, too, the members of my Board. Gentlemen, thank you for your support these many years.

CONTENTS

Foreword. 1

Introduction 5

PART I   **AT WAR WITH THE RULERS OF DARKNESS. . . 13**

CHAPTER 1   The Unseen Enemy 19

CHAPTER 2   Spiritual Hosts of Wickedness. 31

CHAPTER 3   Rulers of the Darkness of This Age 37

PART II   **TIME TO TAKE A STAND!** 45

CHAPTER 4   Principalities and Powers 55

CHAPTER 5   The Accuser 65

PART III   **ANCHOR YOUR LIFE TO THE TRUTH. 75**

CHAPTER 6   The Belt of Truth. 83

CHAPTER 7   What You Don't Know Can Kill You 95

PART IV   **WAGING WAR AGAINST THE ENEMY 103**

CHAPTER 8   A Holy Heart Is a Healthy Heart 111

CHAPTER 9   The Wiles of the Devil. 121

PART V   **KEEPING THE PEACE IN A WORLD WAR 129**

CHAPTER 10   Jesus Won the Day. 135

CHAPTER 11   Christ Our Peace 141

CHAPTER 12   God's Amazing Grace 147

PART VI   YOUR SHIELD OF FAITH ON LIFE'S
                 BATTLEFIELD. 157

CHAPTER 13   Fighting the Good Fight of Faith 165

CHAPTER 14   The Power of Community: Uniting Shields of Faith .173

PART VII   WINNING THE WAR WITHIN. 183

CHAPTER 15   Who's in Charge? God's Chain of Command. 191

CHAPTER 16   Don't Give Place to the Enemy. 199

CHAPTER 17   Holding the High Ground 209

PART VIII   UNLEASHING DIVINE POWER 217

CHAPTER 18   A Two-Edged Sword Cuts Both Ways 225

CHAPTER 19   Time to Go on the Offensive 233

CHAPTER 20   God's Winning Strategy 243

PART IX   THE WARRIOR'S PRAYER. 249

CHAPTER 21   Real-Life Extraterrestrials. 259

CHAPTER 22   Wherever God Marches, Satan Opposes 265

CHAPTER 23   The Value of Prayer Volume 273

FOREWORD

My husband and I make our home just outside of Portland, Oregon. The Pacific Northwest is a wonderland of sorts, long known for its beautiful rivers, tall mountains, and majestic waterfalls. I spent my childhood growing up near the shadow of Mount Hood, but now this place I love has become famous for a different kind of shadow—a spiritual one.

Like many places in the world today, the northwest has found itself at the center of a very real spiritual battle. Take a stroll through the streets of Portland, and you will quickly see the evidence of a city in moral and spiritual crisis. It is impossible to deny the effects of drugs and obvious demonic activity. Ask anyone and they'll tell you that *something* is going on—but you are not likely to find consensus as to what that "something" is.

Charles Spurgeon rightly noted what is really going on when he said, "Consider how precious a soul must be when both God and the devil are after it." He's right, of course. The apostle Paul taught us that we are in a very real spiritual war, and if we're going to be victorious, we need to take our place on the battlefield. It's time we understand who we are as children of God and how to use the weapons God has given us to engage the enemy and defeat him.

As a child of God you really are "armed and dangerous," yet the average Christian has no idea just how heavily armed they are! God has armed you *supernaturally* to win spiritually against a very powerful adversary. In fact, the Bible teaches that "no weapon formed against you will prosper" because ultimately, if you are on the Lord's side, you are on the winning side.

If you're ready to get off the sidelines and take your place on the front lines, the book you are holding in your hand will be of immeasurable help. *The Weapons of our Warfare* **is a handbook for war.** Through the pages of this book, Pastor Phil Hopper helps readers understand why we are going to be victorious, starting with one core truth: we have been given "intel" on our adversary! You see, the good news is that Satan's tactics never change. We know his moves. Second Corinthians 2:11 tells us we *"are not ignorant of his devices."* God has given us vital knowledge in the Bible so we can understand the enemy's tools and the tactics he deploys.

As a former police officer, Phil has a unique perspective on how to engage an enemy, and God is using him to equip and encourage this generation of believers to stand instead of shrink in the face of the struggles we're facing today. Pastor Phil reminds readers that as we prepare to engage the adversary, it's critical that we get our knowledge of the enemy from God's Word and nowhere else. In other words, we need to know our Bible!

As I read this book, my heart was strengthened for battle and my resolve to speak the truth was reinforced. If you need an encourager, you've found one. Pastor Phil will remind you that you are who God says you are—armed by God and a real threat to the enemy. When Satan opposes you, child of God, it is because you are a threat to his dark, shadowy kingdom. Remember, this is light versus darkness, and the good news is *we can win.*

If you've been struggling to get onto the battlefield of culture with courage and confidence, *The Weapons of Our Warfare* is for you. Suit up with the whole armor of God! Don't give up enemy ground—because Christ has won the victory.

Phil's voice is much needed in the Church right now. He is deeply grounded in the rich soil of God's Word, and he'll help you pick up the Sword with the confidence that comes from the Holy Spirit. Phil's humility and kindness is seen each week in the Kansas City area as he brings the Word to his church family at Abundant Life. I have been privileged to sit under his teaching, and I always leave equipped and encouraged. It is on the basis of his character and Christ-likeness that I commend him to you.

Onto the battlefield!

HEIDI ST. JOHN
Tyndale Author and Speaker
Founder, MomStrongInternational.com

INTRODUCTION

A rush of adrenaline coursed through my veins as the dispatcher called my radio number. It was the summer of 1992, and I was a rookie police officer with the Kansas City Missouri Police Department. For the first time, I was patrolling alone without my Field Training Officer. I was finally off "break-in"—no more training wheels. I was now the real deal. I was armed and dangerous, or so I thought.

There was an armed robbery in progress at a nearby convenience store just a few blocks away. This was the call I'd trained for! This was the moment I'd prepared for! I hadn't become a cop to write little old ladies parking tickets. I entered law enforcement because I wanted to catch the real bad guys, and real bad guys were doing really bad things just a few blocks from my location.

I hit the gas and sped to the scene, weaving in and out of traffic. I was determined to get there in time to intercept the perpetrators as they exited the store. I turned the corner in my police cruiser at full speed and skidded into the parking lot on two wheels. My adrenaline was really pumping now!

I screeched my patrol car to a stop along the side of the building and jumped out of the car. I ran to the front of the building, making a strategic approach while staying behind cover like I had been taught. It was then that I reached for the sidearm in my holster. No way was I going to let the bad guys get the drop on me. I would be ready.

I felt for my weapon and suddenly couldn't find that hard, cold metal that had become so familiar to my fingertips. I had practiced drawing my weapon hundreds of times without ever looking down. In combat, you have to keep your eyes up. You can't see the threat coming if you're looking down. By the time you look back up, it could be too late.

When my fingers couldn't find my weapon, my eyes automatically glanced down. To my shock…my weapon wasn't there! My holster was empty! I all but panicked. At any moment, armed robbers would emerge from the store, and I would be in the middle of a violent encounter—unarmed! Lucky for me, instead of the armed robbers bursting from the store, the clerk came walking out. He had heard the commotion announcing my arrival. The bad guys had sped off just moments before I pulled in.

I had made a rookie mistake and one that I will never forget. Earlier in my shift that night, I made an arrest. I correctly followed protocol, locking my gun in the gun locker before booking my arrest into the jail. After completing all the paperwork, I left the police station and went back on patrol, completely forgetting my gun was still locked away safely inside the station. I was instantly humbled by what had happened.

As I drove back to the police station to retrieve my weapon, I contemplated my careless actions. I wasn't feeling "armed and dangerous" like before. The truth is, at that moment, I wasn't dangerous at all because I wasn't armed. I made a mistake that could have cost me my life and the life of that store clerk as well.

I tell you this story because this is the same mistake so many Christians make as they unwittingly go to "war" every day, completely unprepared and completely unarmed. It's not a matter of being careless but rather oblivious to the spiritual battle that rages around us. The apostle Paul warns us in Ephesians 6:12, *"For we do not wrestle against flesh and blood, but against principalities, against powers, against the rulers of the darkness of this age, against spiritual hosts of wickedness in the heavenly places."* We are in a struggle every day with demonic beings–Satan's army of fallen angels. This is not allegory or literary symbolism. This battle is real.

Thankfully, God has equipped us with weapons so we can win. Second Corinthians 10:3-4 tells us, *"For though we walk in the flesh, we do not war according to the flesh. For the weapons of our warfare are not carnal* [physical] *but mighty in God for pulling down strongholds."* We are in a battle that is not physical, it's spiritual, and we have weapons that are not natural—they are supernatural.

> God has armed us supernaturally to win spiritually against a very powerful adversary.

As a child of God, you really are "armed and dangerous." Yet most Christians have no idea just how heavily armed they really are. God has armed us supernaturally to win spiritually against a very powerful adversary. The good news is Satan's tactics never change. We have "intel" on our adversary. We know his moves. Second Corinthians 2:11 tells us we *"are not ignorant of his devices."* Ever since he deceived

Eve into eating of the tree in Genesis 3, he has used the same methods to make war with you and me.

If you want to defeat your enemy, you must first understand his tactics. That is why I wrote my first book, *Defeating the Enemy: Exposing and Overcoming the Strategies of Satan,* in which the strategies Satan uses to try to overcome us are revealed as well as the battle for the Kingdom of God and His throne. Satan hijacked the entire human race when he succeeded in getting Adam to sin with Eve. Because of Adam's sin, every human being since has been born under sin's penalty and Satan's slavery.

Satan hates God. He wants to be worshiped as God and sit on the throne of God. He makes war against the people of God because he knows we are on the earth to advance the Kingdom of God. That is why he is so relentless in his attacks to control, destroy, oppress, overcome, and imprison everyone who professes the name of Christ.

Jesus came to set the captives free—Satan comes to take the free captive.

If you have been born again as a child of the living God, you are a joint heir with Jesus Christ; you are a son or daughter of the King. That means you are under the authority of Jesus and no longer under Satan's authority. Armed with the authority of Jesus, you can have victory and liberty. Jesus says in John 10:10, *"...I have come that they may have life, and that they may have it more abundantly."*

In that same verse, Jesus said Satan is a thief who comes *"to steal, and to kill, and to destroy."* Because he is at war with God, he is at war with the people of God. It is so important that you never go to battle without knowing your enemy—because knowledge is power. God has given us vital knowledge in the Bible so we can understand the enemy's tools and tactics. I encourage you to start your boot camp training as a Kingdom warrior by reading my book, *Defeating the Enemy.* It is an in-depth study of the enemy's strategy that lays the foundation for everything you need to know to effectively put on the whole armor of God.

In *The Weapons of Our Warfare,* we are going beyond a study of the enemy's strategy to a study of our weaponry. God has given us an armory which the apostle Paul has described in Ephesians 6. We must learn both theologically and practically how to use our supernatural weaponry.

I have to warn you—this book is more than just a nice little devotional or motivational pep talk. It's a deeply theological study of Ephesians 6:10-17—the apostle Paul's field manual for believers.

Many years ago, I was issued my weapons as a member of the KCPD Tactical Team (SWAT). Before we fired any of our weapons, we took them apart piece by piece and put them back together again. Our instructors knew it was important for us to become intricately familiar with our weapons and how each part worked.

In the same way, we are going to dissect Ephesians 6:10-17 piece by piece and examine each individual part. Our textbook is the Bible. We are going to learn from God's Word, our ultimate weapon, which is capable of diffusing every situation and defeating every adversary. It's crucial you become intricately familiar with your God-given armor!

Four times in this passage, the apostle Paul tells us to stand against the enemy. However, unless you possess a thorough doctrinal and biblical foundation from our ultimate authority, you will have no strong and stable ground on which to stand. The ground on which most Christians stand is so shaky theologically they can never find consistent victory. They don't know what's true and what's not.

It's crucial you become intricately familiar with your God-given armor!

Paul tells us in Ephesians 4:14, *"No longer be children, tossed to and fro and carried about with every wind of doctrine...."* God wants us to grow to spiritual maturity because otherwise, like a child, we will be easily deceived and defeated by the enemy. This is one of the primary problems in modern Christianity. I have written *The Weapons of Our Warfare* to help Christ followers like you grow in biblical knowledge, which leads to spiritual growth. Like clay in the potter's hand, God's purpose is to mold and shape you into a vessel that cannot be cracked or broken by the threats of the enemy. Instead, you are about to become the adversary's worst nightmare!

The Weapons of Our Warfare is more than a theological dissertation. You are probably not reading it because you want to go to seminary, but because you want to learn how to live in victory daily. How do you navigate the hardships Satan wants to leverage against you as a single mom? How do you overcome the pain and heartache of a loved one's death, a divorce, or financial duress? How do you find peace in the middle of life's storms? My hope is that in the pages that follow you will find practical answers to those questions and much more that will be of value in your everyday walk with the Lord.

As you will discover, one of Satan's strategies is to leverage all of the pain and brokenness of this world to his advantage as he wars against us. But you can win!

As a child of God, you have supernatural weapons; however, many Christians probably don't know how to use them. It's no different than if I was given the keys to an Apache attack helicopter. It is fully equipped for battle with sixteen Hellfire laser-guided missiles, seventy-six 2.75" rockets, and 1,200 rounds of ammunition for its 30mm automatic gun. Now that's power! That's some serious weaponry. However, if it were in my hands, it would be utterly useless. Because I have no training, I wouldn't know how to use it. The best I could hope for would be to not blow myself up!

That's the condition of many Christians who are equipped with powerful weaponry but completely untrained and unprepared for the spiritual combat we all face daily. That, my friend, is about to change.

Even though you are no longer under Satan's slavery, you better take him seriously. First Peter 5:8 says, *"Be sober, be vigilant."* Like Islamic terrorist cells within our own nation, his primary method is one of deception and infiltration. He wants to slip into your life unnoticed, unannounced, and undetected. He is a master illusionist. He is a counterfeiter of all that God is and all that God does.

In my first book, I pulled back the veil of Satan's deception to reveal how Satan uses camouflage to help him blend into his surroundings. He wants to slip into your life unnoticed and unannounced, but Paul reminds us in Second Corinthians 2:11 that we are no longer *"ignorant of his devices."* God has revealed to us through His Word the tools and tactics Satan uses and the devices he deploys. Once you know the weapons of your enemy, it's time to learn about your own.

As a Christian, you are armed and you are dangerous. You may not feel armed and dangerous, but as a child of God, He has given you all the equipment you need to live victoriously against the enemy.

The U.S. military doesn't send soldiers into combat without equipment and the training needed to use it, so we're also going to do a little boot camp training of our own. I'm going to help you learn to use the weapons God has already given you. You're going to learn how to dress for battle, arm yourself, engage in Christian combat, and route the enemy from your home, your family, your workplace—every area of your life.

Am I getting you stirred up? I hope so. My prayer is for this book to equip you to appropriate your victory positionally so you can live it experientially every day and learn what your armor looks like and why it matters.

Get ready to suit up for battle, and get ready to win!

PART I

AT WAR WITH THE RULERS OF DARKNESS

Finally, my brethren, be strong in the Lord and in the power of His might. Put on the whole armor of God, that you may be able to stand against the wiles of the devil. For we do not wrestle against flesh and blood, but against principalities, against powers, against the rulers of the darkness of this age, against spiritual hosts of wickedness in the heavenly place. Therefore take up the whole armor of God, that you may be able to withstand in the evil day, and having done all, to stand. Stand therefore, having girded your waist with truth, having put on the breastplate of righteousness, and having shod your feet with the preparation of the gospel of peace; above all, taking the shield of faith with which you will be able to quench all the fiery darts of the wicked one. And take the helmet of salvation, and the sword of the Spirit, which is the word of God (Ephesians 6:10-17).

The young man suddenly appeared out of nowhere and sat down next to me at the other end of the couch. It was in the fall of 1997, and

I was working off duty at the Marriott in downtown Kansas City. Working an off-duty job is a common practice for those of us in law enforcement. I was picking up a little extra cash by providing security for the hotel. The best part was it afforded me lots of time to quietly sit and think. I was contemplating my future. I was praying and meditating while seeking God's direction for my life. (Don't worry, I was praying with my eyes wide open!)

Was God calling me to leave my career and go into full-time vocational ministry? Several years earlier I had joined the KCPD believing I would have a twenty-five or thirty-year career in law enforcement. Now I sensed maybe God was calling me to preach His Word and minister the gospel on a full-time basis. It was a big decision that would completely change the direction of my life, and I didn't want to get it wrong.

When the young man suddenly appeared and sat down, he leaned forward for a few seconds, putting his head in his hands. Then he sat back, looked directly at me, and asked, "Do you know the purpose of life?" I sat there a bit stunned and remember saying, "No, what is it?" To which he responded, "The purpose of life is to know God and make God known." With that said, he stood up and disappeared around the corner.

He had no sooner left when my spirit leapt inside of me! I thought, *Who was that guy? Where did he come from? Wait, I want to talk to you some more!* I jumped off the couch just moments after this mysterious individual abruptly departed. With three quick steps, I was at the corner, fully expecting to see him walking down the long corridor where I could catch up to him and talk to him some more. But he was gone.

He had vanished. There were no doors on either side of the corridor. No exits. There was nowhere he could have gone. There was no way he could have made it to the end of that long, empty hallway. He had literally disappeared into thin air. I was convinced right then and there that God had sent an angel to minister His message to me. The purpose of my life was to "know God and make God known." It is a mission I have devoted every day of my life to since that day in 1997.

GOD'S MESSENGERS

Who and what are angels? Hebrews 1:14 says, *"Are they not all ministering spirits sent forth to minister for those who will inherit salvation?"* From this verse, we learn that angels, among other things, are God's servants and messengers that He dispatches to minister to *"those who will inherit salvation."*

While God's angels are messengers and ministers, so are Satan's. Paul says in Second Corinthians 12:7, *"...a thorn in the flesh was given to me, a messenger of Satan to buffet me...."* Angels are messengers of God, but in Paul's case, he encountered a messenger of Satan. Angels are ministers of good or evil, depending on who they are working for. One of Satan's angels had been assigned to Paul to afflict and buffet him. This demonic messenger was there to minister evil to Paul, yet Paul knew that God would use it for good.

It's important to remember that angels don't always take on the form of a human to minister to us, but the Bible absolutely teaches they can:

> *Do not forget to entertain strangers, for by so doing some have unwittingly entertained angels* (Hebrews 13:2).

Imagine the implications! You could be interacting with somebody who looks like a human, but the entire time it is actually an angel that has taken on the form of a human being. We can see this pattern repeatedly in Scripture.

Genesis 18–19 is a remarkable story of how God sent angels in preparation for His destruction of Sodom and Gomorrah because of the sin and wickedness of those cities. In Genesis 18:2, Abraham looked up and saw three *"men"* standing before him. Although the Bible calls them men, we quickly learn they were more than mere men. Abraham immediately rose up, ran to them, bowed down, and called one of them "Lord." He recognized one of these *"men"* as the Angel of the Lord, the pre-incarnate Lord Jesus Christ and began to worship Him.

In Genesis 18:4, Abraham washed their feet; in verse 5, he offered them food; in verse 7, he killed *"a tender and good calf"* and prepared to honor them with a feast. These angels had taken on the form of human beings with human bodies that were capable of biological functions like eating food. When you read the entire text, you learn that the *"man"* referred to as the Lord stayed back with Abraham as recorded in Genesis 18:22, while the other two *"men"* went down to Sodom.

Genesis 19:1 records, *"Now the two angels came to Sodom in the evening, and Lot was sitting in the gate of Sodom...."* These two "men" are called angels, yet they look like human men to the wicked citizens of Sodom. Abraham's nephew, Lot, brought them into his house for the night because they obviously looked like men. Genesis 19:4-5 continues:

> *Now before they lay down, the men of the city, the men of Sodom, both old and young, all the people from every quarter, surrounded the house. And they called to Lot and said to him, "Where are the men who came to you tonight? Bring them out to us that we may know them carnally."*

What was it this wicked mob of men wanted to do with these two "men" they had seen go into Lot's house? Well, I'll give you a hint. They didn't want them to come outside so they could all roast marshmallows together around a campfire. Had these two men not really been angels that supernaturally blinded the men of the city (Genesis 19:11), the entire mob would have sexually assaulted and raped them. I'm not trying to be graphic, just real. Angels have the ability to take on the appearance of human beings with fully functioning human bodies. Hebrews 13:2 confirms that *"some have unwittingly entertained angels."*

Angels are always described as male throughout the pages of the Bible. I know this blows away the images of the plump porcelain-skinned little cherubs fluttering about with stubby little wings while plucking little harps, but that imagery has been formed in our imagination by pop culture. The Bible paints a much different picture. The Bible always describes angels as masculine creatures. This is contrary to our politically correct, gender-neutral world. I would rather be biblically correct than politically correct.

To many in our modern world, this all sounds crazy. The idea of angels interacting with humans or the idea of the unseen realm materializing into the physical realm seems more like a sci-fi movie. Even among Christians, there is a tendency to try to take the supernatural out of the Bible and explain everything through a naturalistic lens. It is how we are conditioned as Westerners. Much of the worldview of Western civilization is built on naturalism, rationalism, and intellectualism. We aren't a superstitious people. We're sophisticated and educated, which is why the tendency even among today's Christians is to explain away the supernatural elements of the Bible.

Even trained theologians and Bible scholars routinely attempt to remove the supernatural from the Bible. As my congregation has heard me say many times, "The Bible is not hard to understand, just sometimes hard to believe." It's hard to believe because our rational minds are conditioned to explain everything we see, hear, and experience through a naturalistic filter. The Bible teaches something different altogether. There is the natural world but also the supernatural world. There is the physical realm but also the spiritual realm. There is the realm we can see, as well as the unseen realm, and the two intersect on a daily basis.

This is why the apostle Paul writes in Ephesians 6:12, *"We do not wrestle against flesh and blood, but…against the rulers of the darkness of this age…."*

CHAPTER 1

THE UNSEEN ENEMY

For we do not wrestle against flesh and blood, but against principalities, against powers, against the rulers of the darkness of this age, against spiritual hosts of wickedness in the heavenly places (Ephesians 6:12).

Who are these rulers of darkness? They are the unseen enemy. God has an angel army, and Satan does too. Paul is telling us we are locked in a struggle with demons, *"spiritual hosts of wickedness in the heavenly places."* They are the fallen angels that rebelled with Satan, and Paul says we wrestle with them daily.

While God's angels can and do take on human form as illustrated by the story of Genesis 18–19, Satan's angels can as well. (Now wait…take a deep breath before you march next door and accuse your neighbor of being a demon!) Most of the time Satan's demonic army prefers to work in the unseen realm. In our Western culture, they especially prefer to launch their attacks while never being noticed, seen, or suspected. Most Americans don't believe in Satan or demons, and that is exactly how Satan wants it. Even most Christians, while perhaps believing in Satan and demons theologically, don't really believe they affect their daily lives practically.

We read the gospel accounts of how Jesus routinely interacted with the demonic. And in the book of Acts, we see how Paul and the apostles encountered the demonic consistently, and then either consciously or subconsciously we think to ourselves, *Well, that stuff just happened back then, but it doesn't now.*

"I need you to call me quickly, I'm dealing with a spirit of suicide."

"I need you to call me quickly, I'm dealing with a spirit of suicide." That was the text I received a while back from a member of our ministry team I'll call "Kathy." She was ministering to a woman I'll call "Sarah," who had only a few weeks earlier placed her faith in Jesus and was now a new Christian. When I called Kathy, she began describing what her new disciple was going through. Sarah was suicidal almost every night and had been for many years. It began when she was a teenager. She had been sexually molested repeatedly beginning when she was only five years of age. The sexual abuse continued through her teen years and even into her adult years.

For years, Sarah saw what seemed like a dark shadow that appeared in her bedroom at night and attached itself to her. She would be filled with a feeling of hopelessness and doom. She had made several attempts to take her life over the years, and she had been in and out of multiple mental health programs and hospitals. She spent years taking various medications for depression and mental illness. She also received counseling and psychotherapy, but nothing helped.

I immediately went to Kathy's home and listened to Sarah's story. I explained that I thought she was battling a demon. She had come to faith in Christ and had received the Spirit of God. People who are born again of God's Spirit cannot be possessed by an evil spirit, but because Sarah had just come to faith in Christ, this spiritual confrontation was imminent. There were spiritual powers at war for control of her life.

I asked Sarah if she believed Jesus had the power to set her free. She indicated she did. I prayed over Sarah and then looked at her and said, "Sarah, say this with me, 'Jesus set me free.'" As soon as I did, her mouth and jaw clenched tightly shut, and she began to shake. I knew I was dealing directly with a demon, but I never had a class on "How to Cast Out a Demon."

Although I had never directly encountered this kind of situation before, I was confident in my Kingdom authority as a child of God. I recalled what Jesus said in Luke 10:19, *"Behold, I give you the authority to trample on serpents and scorpions, and over all the power of the enemy...."* I kept encouraging Sarah to say, "Jesus, set me free." I could see her trying to move her lips, but her jaw was clenched shut. Something was holding her mouth shut. I repeated to Sarah, "Say, 'Jesus set me free,'" while Kathy and another ministry partner continued praying for her. Sarah just continued to clench her mouth shut and shake.

This had been going on for several minutes when the Holy Spirit told me what to do. I said, "Demonic spirit, in the name of Jesus identify yourself. What is your name?" Immediately Sarah opened her mouth, and the word "death" came out. It was a spirit of death. I commanded the spirit of death to come out of Sarah in Jesus' name. Suddenly she sat back in her chair and stopped shaking. Her body relaxed and her eyes were now open for the first time in several minutes. As she looked at me, I said, "Sarah, tell me how you feel right now." With a smile beginning to crease her mouth, she said the word "free." She was free.

We all began to pray together and sing praises to our Savior! I left that night believing Sarah had been delivered from the jaws of the enemy. And she had. What I didn't know was there were yet more.

"Come quickly, there are more demons Sarah is dealing with!"

"Come quickly, there are more demons Sarah is dealing with!" That was the text I received the next day, and fortunately, I was nearby. I arrived minutes later and walked into the room in time to see Kathy bandaging Sarah's arm. Sarah was clearly in a trance-like condition. Kathy told me that as she was again ministering God's Word to Sarah, she went into a trance-like state and without warning pulled out a box-cutter-type razor blade from her pocket and began slashing her arm repeatedly. Kathy had been able to wrestle the razor blade away from Sarah. (One more reason to never do this alone. Remember, in Luke 10, Jesus sent out the disciples in pairs.)

We commanded this demon to identify itself, and when Sarah opened her mouth, the word "self-hatred" came out. It was a demon of self-hatred. Once again I said to Sarah, "Say, 'Jesus set me free.'" As soon as I did, the same thing happened as it had the night before. Her jaw clenched shut, and her lips were sealed tight. I could see her trying to move her mouth, but she clearly could not. Something was holding it shut as her body shook. We commanded the spirit of self-hatred to depart in Jesus' name.

At one point, Sarah raised her fist above her head and began to beat herself violently. I noted that as she beat herself, her arm was not moving in a natural motion, but rather in a mechanical robotic type movement. Clearly, something other than Sarah was controlling her arm. We continued commanding the spirit to depart in Jesus' name, and within minutes Sarah sat back, and her body relaxed. We knew it was gone and Sarah did too. She was back. This time we asked Sarah if she thought there were more. And there were…

Over the next thirty days, Sarah was delivered from no less than twenty demons identifying themselves with names like shame, fear, lies, deceit, despair, and murder, just to name a few, besides death and self-hatred that were identified early on. Today Sarah is still part of our church, and she is living spiritually free. She has had no relapses and has not been suicidal or had any symptoms of mental illness since that life-changing encounter with the power of Jesus! She admits that when she is not renewing her mind in the Word and renouncing the lies with the Truth, she can feel the darkness encroaching on her once again. But now she knows what to do.

Now I have to tell you, since this encounter with Sarah, I have shared this story with a number of pastors of several different Bible-believing churches who have asked me privately for my theological opinion on the work of demons and deliverance ministry as a whole. Each of these pastors came from theologically conservative traditions, meaning they fully believe in the authority and inerrancy of the Bible. None would doubt the existence of either Satan or demons.

Yet only one of them has had a similar experience in his pastoral ministry and nodded in affirmation as I recounted the story. All the rest looked at me and said something like, "Phil, if it was anyone other than you telling me this story, I'd think they were crazy." Why? Why would even pastors and teachers of God's Word think it's crazy to encounter demons in a real, tangible way when both the Old and New Testaments are full of passages that clearly articulate the reality of the demonic?

WHY THE SKEPTICISM?

I know the answer to that question. I know why even pastors have a hard time believing a story like this when they hear it from another pastor whom they know isn't crazy and is quite conservative theologically. The reason I know the answer is because at one time my response would have been just like theirs.

The first reason is how the subject of the demonic has been sensationalized and dramatized by those in the Church who frankly want to make it all about them and put on the biggest show in town. It's nothing more than an attention getter. Many have seen the circus many churches have become when their leaders are all about the hype. Most of us, including myself, are not interested in the "circus" that sometimes follows deliverance ministries. As a result, many in the Church have become jaded by the constant implications that the demonic might be closer than we think, and we are called to be the weapons in God's hands to confront the darkness.

> We are called to be the weapons in God's hands to confront the darkness.

There is another reason why so many in the Church are reluctant to recognize demonic influences. It is church culture and church tradition. I came from a church tradition and was raised in a church culture that would have certainly believed theologically in the existence of the demonic. But for some reason, while that church tradition acknowledged demons theologically, they refused to acknowledge demons practically. I remember receiving very little teaching on the demonic, and I was a kid raised in Sunday school. I've spent my entire life in church. I heard hundreds of sermons before I ever preached my first one. Until I preached on the subject of spiritual warfare myself, I'm not sure I had ever actually heard a single sermon, much less a whole sermon series, on the subject or the work of Satan in our lives as he wars against us.

Our Westernized Christianity gives many in the body of Christ a naturalistic filter, especially when we encounter the supernatural. Our rational minds are trained to immediately dismiss anything that doesn't fit within the natural and the physical.

I think somewhere along the way many pastors, churches, and Christians have adopted the "wasp theology" on Satan. When I was a little boy and a wasp would fly nearby, I would get anxious. I knew that a wasp has a stinger on the tail and could inflict some serious pain. But I remember my mom always saying, "Don't worry. If you don't bother it, it won't bother you." For some reason, my approach to avoid getting stung by a wasp became my theology for not getting stung by Satan. "If I ignore him, he'll ignore me."

I believe that's what many others in the body of Christ think as well. Subtly, without any real direct teaching on the subject, I was taught to not even acknowledge Satan. I think in an effort to not *give place to the devil*" (Ephesians 4:27), I was taught to make no mention of the devil and give him no thought or attention. This is hardly a winning strategy when you consider the words of Paul in Ephesians 6:12, *"We do not wrestle against flesh and blood, but against principalities, against powers, against the rulers of the darkness of this age."*

> ## Whether or not you're paying attention to him, the enemy is paying attention to you.

Whether or not you're paying attention to him, the enemy is paying attention to you. If you're not aware of Satan's interest in you, you are already his prisoner in at least some fashion and probably a prisoner unaware! If God didn't want us to be aware of the demons or to actively engage them in warfare, then the Holy Spirit would have never inspired Paul to pen Ephesians 6:10-17 that describes the armor of God.

FROM GOD'S WORD ONLY

Now I have to warn you—it's critical you get this knowledge of the enemy from God's Word and nowhere else. God has already revealed everything you need to know in the Bible. The word "occult" means secret or esoteric knowledge and includes anything related to the worship of or communion with secret powers or spirits through psychics, New Age mysticism, participation in séances for the purpose of communicating with the dead, spiritism, sorcery, Wicca, witchcraft, palm readers, tarot cards, fortune tellers, Ouija boards, voodoo, the zodiac, astrology and more. These and other practices were forbidden by God as His people were preparing to enter the Promised Land. They were going to encounter pagan people who practiced them (Deuteronomy 18:9-12).

It's true that many of the people who practice these things today are nothing more than fakes and phonies who only want your money. It's equally true that the practices themselves are not fake and not phony. This is real, and it's not a game. You may take a trip to the psychic fair and hang a crystal from the rear-view mirror—and if you do, you're apt to come home with a demon sitting in the back seat of your car. God forbids these kinds of practices because they are the "welcome mat" to the door of your home. They are the doorway of the demonic into your life.

You may get that secret knowledge, but you will get it like Eve got hers when she ate of the tree in Genesis 3. She got that knowledge all right and a whole lot more! You should even beware of the movies you watch and the music you listen to. Anything that glorifies the darkness or the demonic is something that has the power to give the enemy access into your life.

I'm convinced now after years of studying the Word and years of pastoral ministry, that there are scores of demonized people walking among us every day. And there are scores of demonized people walking into our churches every week. I don't mean all of them are demonically possessed, though that's probably more common than most of us can imagine. The Greek words *daimon* and *daimonion* appear dozens of times in the New Testament and are commonly translated as demon. The verb form of *daimonion* is *daimonizo* and occurs around twelve times in the New Testament. Our English equivalent is *demonize* meaning someone who is demonized or "has a demon."

The Collins English Dictionary defines *demonize* as "to subject to demonic influence." Defined in this manner, it's safe to say we have all been demonized at some time in our lives. There are different levels of demonization. Not every demonized person is as demonized as Sarah had been for most of her life until those glorious thirty days when Jesus set her free. Demonization can imply anything from demonic possession, oppression, manipulation, or affliction. It can, but does not always, imply complete control or domination by a demon. It can also imply far lesser forms of influence.

By definition, the apostle Paul himself was demonized. He acknowledged suffering from demonic affliction as recorded in Second Corinthians 12:7. While I'm personally convinced a believer indwelt by God's Spirit (Romans 8:9) cannot simultaneously be possessed by an evil spirit, I'm also convinced believers can be demonically oppressed, controlled, or manipulated if they are unrepentant of sin or unsubmitted to the lordship of Christ at any time in their lives. This is why Ephesians 4:27 says, *Don't give place to the devil.* The devil has lost all place in your life as a born-again child of God. Sin, however, returns control to him. Embracing a lie instead of the truth can give him a foothold, and that foothold can become a demonic stronghold (2 Corinthians 10:4).

> The devil has no place in your life as a born-again child of God.

This is probably the condition of many Christians suffering under varying levels of demonic control. Knowing what I know now, there were times in my pastoral ministry over the years when I counseled someone who was demonized. I wish I would have known back then what I know now. I wish I would have had the spiritual insight back then to more effectively help them.

I recall praying for several different people in counseling sessions on several different occasions. On each occasion, I was praying over them and for them and invoking Jesus' name against any demonic power or principality that might have been afflicting them. As I was praying, they began hyperventilating and shaking to the point I thought I was going to have to summon an ambulance. But as I kept praying, they suddenly slumped back in their chair, relaxed their body, and their breathing returned to normal. I don't know for sure, but I think it's possible on these occasions I had cast out a demon without even knowing it. I didn't know then what I know now.

What I do know now is to take seriously and literally what Paul reminds us of in Second Corinthians 10:3, *"For though we walk in the flesh, we do not war according to the flesh."*

CHAPTER 2

SPIRITUAL HOSTS OF WICKEDNESS

For we do not wrestle against flesh and blood, but against principalities, against powers, against the rulers of the darkness of this age, against spiritual hosts of wickedness in the heavenly places (Ephesians 6:12).

When you understand the devil's tactics I exposed in *Defeating the Enemy,* you are ready to examine what the apostle Paul says about putting on the full armor of God, learning how to wage warfare, and living in victory. In chapter 6 of the book of Ephesians, Paul describes how we can effectively wage warfare against the spiritual world that is just as real as the world we can see with our physical eyes.

In Ephesians 6:10-11, Paul tells us, *"Finally... be strong in the Lord and in the power of His might. Put on the whole armor of God, that you may be able to stand against the wiles* [or schemes] *of the devil."* Clearly Satan, or more specifically members of his demonic army, are scheming against us. The apostle Paul described them as *"spiritual hosts of wickedness in the heavenly places."* What does this mean?

Paul tells us in Romans 1:20 that everything God has created in the physical world is a reflection of what is already a very real part of the spiritual world. In other words, what can be known spiritually—the unseen—can be known through what we can see physically—the seen. *God created everything we see physically to give us a picture of everything spiritually that we cannot see.*

STARS AND ANGELS

The Bible teaches the stars of the heavens are symbolic of angels. Revelation 12:4, Revelation 1:20, and other passages tell us that when you look up at the night sky and see the stars, they are symbols of angels to remind us of the angelic world. Psalm 147:4 tells us God has numbered all the stars, and He knows them all by name. Romans 1:20 says that everything in God's physical creation is a picture of something that is true spiritually. Why would God number and name all the stars? I believe it is possible that every star represents a specific angel.

We don't know how many stars there are, but astronomers say there could be as many as seventy-seven sextillion. That's a number beyond our ability to even comprehend. What we can comprehend is there are a whole lot of angels, and there are far more of them than there are of us.

Stars are meant to give light; however, remember there are angels of light as well as angels of darkness and the rulers of the darkness of this age. These are the angels that used to give light but were judged by God for their rebellion with darkness. Could it be that a black hole reflects an angel that used to be an angel of light but is now an angel of darkness and a ruler of darkness? A black hole is simply a star that has died. It used to give light, but now all it gives is darkness. In fact, its gravitational pull swallows all the light that goes near it. Think about that! It is no coincidence that ancient civilizations around the world have all worshiped the stars, and many people continue to do so to this day.

From the beginning of his rebellion described in Isaiah 14:12, Satan has always wanted to be worshiped as God. He always counterfeits the worship of God. That is why many have worshiped the stars, representing the angelic world and the cosmos from which the spiritual hosts of wickedness in the heavenly places reign.

Not only are stars symbolic of angels throughout Scripture, but Job 38:7 calls angels *"stars"* or *"morning stars."* It's beginning to make more sense why God has numbered and named all the stars and why people historically have worshiped the stars in the night sky. Job 38:7 tells us that as God was creating the world and laying its foundation, the *"morning stars sang together, and all the sons of God shouted for joy."*

Who are these *"sons of God"* known as *"morning stars"?* They can't be humans. Adam's race hadn't been created yet. For God was only at that moment creating the foundations of the world. They are clearly a type of angel. Perhaps they are a high-ranking class of angels or cherubs that witnessed God's miraculous creative work as He laid the foundations of the world. They worshiped God, singing for joy at what they witnessed Him doing.

> *God stands in the congregation of the mighty; He judges among the gods. How long will you judge unjustly, and show partiality to the wicked?* (Psalm 82:1-2)

Psalm 82 is a biblical text that blows to pieces the theological box most of us have. It helps us see into the unseen realm if we're willing to open our spiritual eyes to the truth. In verse 1, the Hebrew word *elohim* occurs twice in that single short verse. Other than God's covenant name Yahweh, it is the word used most often in the Old Testament for God. The word *elohim* is most often used as God's personal name, which is how it's used the first time it appears in Psalm 82:1. It can also refer to a whole pantheon of "gods" as it is used the second time at the end of Psalm 82:1. The word *elohim* is like a lot of our English words. The same word can be used for the singular or plural, and the context and grammar make it clear which one is being used. The word "sheep" can refer to a single sheep or a whole flock of sheep. So it is with the word *elohim*.

In Psalm 82:1, we find God *(Elohim)* meeting with an entire assembly of "gods" *(elohim)*. The context of Psalm 82 is God judging an assembly of "gods" for their corrupt administration of the nations. Most theological commentators offer really flimsy explanations for what is written in Psalm 82. They believe the "gods" are actually just Jewish elders and mere men, or it is evidence of the Trinity. How silly. Nowhere has God ever assigned a council of Jewish elders to reign over foreign nations, and it's ludicrous to think God the Father is reprimanding the other members of the Trinity—God the Son and God the Spirit.

These answers are just not honest about the straightforward nature of the text and are offered only because they don't fit our theological box. Thank you Mr. Theologian, but please don't protect us from the truth. We can handle it.

Most Christian theologians and commentators avoid the obvious in Psalm 82 because to admit there are other "gods" besides our God would appear to support polytheism, the belief in many gods.

That would be heresy, but that is not at all what the writer of Psalm 82 is doing.

All the writers of the Old Testament were monotheists, one of the hallmarks of the ancient Jews. They believed in only one God as recorded in Deuteronomy 6:4: *"Hear, O Israel: The Lord our God, the Lord is one!"* God was declaring there is no other God but the God of Israel. God was preparing His people to go into Canaan where they would be completely surrounded by pagan people with many gods. While reminding them that He alone is the only true God, Maker, and Creator, He warns them in Deuteronomy 6:14, *"You shall not go after other gods, the gods of the people who are all around you."* These would be among the gods referred to in Psalm 82:1. They are the *"sons of God"* and *"morning stars,"* originally referred to in Job 38:7. Some of them would join an angelic rebellion against God and seek to be worshiped as God.

Here's the point: Like many millions around the world today, the ancient pagans all worshiped false gods. They were not and are not merely figments of their imaginations, as many of us have been led to believe. Somewhere buried beneath the mythology of pagan belief systems is the truth of other god-like beings in the universe that God had created. They were supposed to give God worship but instead desired to be worshiped themselves.

The Canaanites worshiped Baal and Ashtoreth among many others. The Egyptians worshiped gods like Ra, Nut, Osiris, and Isis. The Greeks worshiped many gods, including Zeus, Poseidon, Athena, and Aphrodite. The Romans worshiped Jupiter, Venus, and Apollo among others. None of these gods were just imaginary deities. These ancient people worshiped them because they were all very powerful god-like beings that had rebelled against the God who created them and made them, the One they had witnessed creating and laying the foundations of the earth.

Remember, Satan's desire has always been to steal the worship of God and the throne of God. These gods, and many others that have historically been worshiped, are the sons of God and the morning stars in Job 38:7. With Satan's insurrection, some rebelled against God and now seek to rule the nations in opposition to God. In Psalm 82, God is standing in the midst of their assembly promising judgment and destruction on them for their corrupt administration of the nations. They were once rulers in God's Kingdom of light but are now rulers in Satan's kingdom of darkness.

CHAPTER 3

RULERS OF THE DARKNESS OF THIS AGE

For we do not wrestle against flesh and blood, but against principalities, against powers, against the rulers of the darkness of this age, against spiritual hosts of wickedness in the heavenly places (Ephesians 6:12).

What does it mean to say we wrestle against an unseen enemy, the rulers of the darkness of this age? What is it we are wrestling for and why are we at war? As I wrote in *Defeating the Enemy,* we know the angelic race was on the earth before the human race. Before Adam was in the Garden of Eden, there was a being known as the *"anointed cherub"* (Ezekiel 28:14). He reigned on the earth from *"Eden, the garden of*

God" (Ezekiel 28:13). Before Adam's race was ever created, the angels reigned on the earth. It was an angelic kingdom with their leader, the anointed cherub, reigning over them and with them. Before Satan rebelled against God, he reigned over the morning stars and other sons of God. The earth was their home and Eden was his throne.

We don't know how long they were here before Adam's creation or what else was here, other than what we learn from Ezekiel 28. What we do know is there was a day when the anointed cherub looked up into heaven and challenged God to war!

> *How you are fallen from heaven, O Lucifer, son of the morning! How you are cut down to the ground, you who weakened the nations! For you have said in your heart: "I will ascend into heaven, I will exalt my throne above the stars of God; I will also sit on the mount of the congregation on the farthest sides of the north; I will ascend above the heights of the clouds, I will be like the Most High"* (Isaiah 14:12-14).

Lucifer, whose name means shining one or light bearer, says five rebellious "I will" statements beginning with *"I will ascend into heaven."* He had to ascend into heaven because he was somewhere below heaven. He was on the earth. He looked up from his earthly throne where he reigned over an earthly kingdom and was consumed with jealousy. He wanted God's heavenly throne. He and his rebellious angel army were thrown out of heaven, the dwelling place of God, into the heavenlies, or cosmos.

God judged the anointed cherub with darkness. If *"God is light and in Him is no darkness at all"* according to First John 1:5, then where did the darkness come from in Genesis 1:2? Darkness is not an attribute of God but rather of sin and Satan. By Genesis 1:2, Lucifer had sinned and God had judged the "light bearer" with darkness. He had now become the one we know as Satan, the leader of the rulers of the darkness. He and the multitude of morning stars that rebelled with him continue to this day to make their abode in the cosmos. Paul describes them as spiritual hosts of wickedness in the heavenly places. More to come about this in the next section.

What is clear is that after God judged Satan with darkness, he wanted to reclaim what was once his—dominion of the earth. The problem for the fallen cherub was that God had replaced him with a completely new creation. God gave this new creation His own image and likeness, making Him a triune being like Him. God called this new being Adam or man and put him in the very same garden from which the fallen cherub used to reign as the anointed cherub (Genesis 2:7-8).

Worst of all, God had given this new creature dominion over the earth and a commission to be fruitful and multiply and fill the earth. If the fallen cherub didn't work fast, there would soon be hundreds of thousands of God's image bearers all over the earth establishing an earthly kingdom as God intended. Where the angelic race once reigned, Adam's race would now reign instead. Adam had dominion over Satan's old home and would forever reign from his old throne, so the fallen cherub had to move fast!

What happened in Genesis 3? Adam sinned and rebelled against God. He died spiritually and lost the perfect image of God in which he had been created. He lost the image of God, he lost the title of son of God, and worst of all he lost the Kingdom of God because he could no longer reproduce the image of God. He could only reproduce the image of a fallen man (Genesis 5:3). When Adam sinned, dominion of the earth was passed back to the fallen cherub now known as Satan.

Here's the point: Where Adam's race was originally intended to reign on the earth under the throne of God, Satan and his rebellious army of fallen angels now rule instead.

The consequences were catastrophic for Adam's race. First John 5:19 says, *"The whole world lies under the sway* [power] *of the wicked one."* Second Corinthians 4:4 calls Satan the *"god of this age,"* and Ephesians 6:12 calls his angel army the *"rulers of the darkness of this age."* It is in this current age that Satan and his demonic princes rule the kingdoms of the world.

This is why Satan could tempt Jesus in Matthew 4:8-9 by offering Him all the kingdoms of the world if He would only fall down and worship him. Others have scoffed at Satan from this passage saying, "He couldn't even offer the kingdoms to Jesus. They didn't belong to him—they belonged to God." But that is not what Jesus said! Jesus didn't scoff at him, reprimand him, or correct him because Jesus knew the kingdoms of this world were rightfully Satan's. That right had been legally transferred to him when Adam sinned and lost dominion.

Unlike the first Adam, the second "Adam"—Jesus—didn't take Satan's bait (1 Corinthians 15:45). Jesus fully understood God's plan to restore His authority on earth if He did it God's way instead of Satan's way.

When our resurrected and rightful King returns to reclaim the earth for Adam's race, He will rule finally and forever all the kingdoms of this world. And we, as the redeemed of Adam's race, will reign with Him. Jesus is coming back with a scroll secured by seven seals—the title deed to the earth. He's going to say to a counterfeit king known as Satan, "I have the title deed in hand, now get off My land!"

And they sang a new song, saying: "You are worthy to take the scroll, and to open its seals; for you were slain, and have redeemed us to God by Your blood out of every tribe and tongue and people and nation, and have made us kings and priests to our God; and we shall reign on the earth" (Revelation 5:9-10).

As the redeemed of God, one day we will reign as kings and priests just as God planned when He created Adam, placed him in the Garden, and said to *"be fruitful and multiply; fill the earth."*

The plan God had for Adam has been delayed by sin, but it has not been destroyed by sin.

As members of God's Kingdom, having been redeemed from Satan's kingdom, we are locked in mortal combat with a very real and powerful adversary who wants nothing more than to advance his kingdom in opposition to God's. As a child of God, you pose a threat to his kingdom and he wants to take you out.

You don't need to be threatened by Satan, but you should take him seriously because he is ready to strike the moment you let your guard down. Many Christians I know walk around in constant fear of the devil. I hear them say, "I'm just being attacked by Satan!" as if they are completely at Satan's mercy and there is nothing they can do about it. Yes, we are being attacked almost every day by the devil's perversions on television, in the movie theater, on social media, and pop culture just to name a few of his diabolical devices.

This satanic spirit that is anti-Christ is everywhere in society. Our minds are constantly being bombarded by the lies, the sin, and the depravity of the enemy. Other times we take a direct hit by one of the *"fiery darts of the wicked one"* (Ephesians 6:16), which we will learn more about later. In whatever form the attack comes, it's crucial to remember who our real adversary is. It's never the one you can see but rather the one that is unseen, or as Paul puts it, *"We do not wrestle against flesh and blood."*

Paul is saying your real enemy is not your boss on Monday morning with whom you can't get along. Your real enemy is not your coworker across the cubicle who just seems to afflict you and torment you and get under your skin. Your real enemy is not your ex-spouse. Satan can and does use people to afflict you, but Paul is saying that your real enemy is not the one you can see. Your real enemy is the one behind the scenes pulling the strings. This is not a physical battle but rather one that is spiritual in nature.

Here's the point: As a child of God, you don't have to fear Satan. He fears you!

Satan fears you because he knows what you are capable of if you ever realize the power and authority you have in Christ. He fears what you can accomplish. He fears you because you are a threat to him and his kingdom.

As mortal human beings, we are no match against the power of Satan. To oppose him in our own strength and in our own power is a suicide mission. Thanks be to God our victory over the enemy does not come by our own strength but through Christ's power and authority alone. That's why Paul says in Ephesians 6:10 to *"be strong in the Lord and in the power of His might."* It's quite logical to assume that in our own strength and power, as mortal creatures, we have no strength against the power of Satan.

Christ has the greatest strength, power, and authority in the entire universe.

The Bible tells us in Romans 8:37 that in the strength of Jesus Christ and the power of the living God, *"we are more than conquerors."* You don't have to be conquered. You are more than a victor; you don't have to live like a victim. In John 16:33, Jesus says you can be an overcomer and not only survive—but thrive! Even if you are caught in any number of Satan's snares and strongholds, you can break free because Christ has the greatest strength, power, and authority in the entire universe. And it is time to take a stand!

PART II

TIME TO TAKE A STAND!

*Finally, my brethren, be strong in the Lord and in the power of His might. Put on the whole armor of God, that you may be able to **stand** against the wiles of the devil. For we do not wrestle against flesh and blood, but against principalities, against powers, against the rulers of the darkness of this age, against spiritual hosts of wickedness in the heavenly places. Therefore take up the whole armor of God, that you may be able to withstand in the evil day, and having done all, to **stand. Stand** therefore, having girded your waist with truth, having put on the breastplate of righteousness, and having shod your feet with the preparation of the gospel of peace; above all, taking the shield of faith with which you will be able to quench all the fiery darts of the wicked one. And take the helmet of salvation, and the sword of the Spirit, which is the word of God* (Ephesians 6:10-17).

Here I was in one of my least favorite places on earth, circling the crowded parking lot of a popular shopping destination. It was right before Christmas, and it was packed with cars and people. Parking spots were at a premium. My kids were much younger then, so I was driving a practical set of wheels—a minivan I affectionately dubbed the "man van." I knew it didn't do anything to help my image. I had gotten over the need to drive a cool car for the sake of my image many years before.

Suddenly, a car pulled out right in front of me, and I had to lock up my brakes to keep from running into it. It was a compact 4-cylinder with a spoiler on the back and low-profile wheels. Somebody was trying hard to make a Honda Civic look fast and cool. *None of my business,* I thought to myself, *somebody must have an insecure self-image.* But the car didn't move out of the way; it just sat there in front of me. I looked inside and could see the driver staring at me. He was giving me the "mean mug."

Wait a minute, I thought. *This guy pulls out in front of me. I have to slam on my brakes to avoid hitting him, and now he's staring me down as if I've done something wrong? I don't think so.*

As a former cop, let's just say I know how to quickly size people up. He was a kid, maybe nineteen or twenty years of age, around 5' 9" and 145 pounds. He was clearly trying to act tough and intimidate me. I knew he was just a wannabe. He wasn't really tough, and he really wasn't a threat. He was just a young kid.

Most of the time I would have just politely waved or patiently waited for him to make his point and then move on. But I didn't this time. Maybe I was tired, or maybe my patience was already on empty from the overcrowded parking lot. Either way, I decided this day to teach the kid a lesson.

So I stared back at him. I didn't blink. I just stared right back at him and mimicked the same look he was giving me. He then tried to look even meaner. I mirrored his look again. He then shrugged his shoulders and raised his hands as if to say, "You want some of this?" So I made the exact same gesture, shrugging my shoulders and raising my hands as if to say, "Do you want some of this?" He then glanced at the passenger in his car. Clearly, his machismo was on the line. What would he do now that his bravado had been challenged?

He made one last effort to save his ego and jumped out of his car. It was then that my police training kicked in—never allow someone to approach while you're sitting in your car. Get out of your car to meet the threat. I jumped out of the "man van," standing behind the driver's door and stopped him in his tracks. What he saw while I'd been sitting down was an old man in a minivan. What he couldn't tell while I was sitting down was that the old man in the minivan was actually 6' 6" tall and could still bench-press well over 350 pounds.

In my police voice, I said, "Man, get back in your car, you ain't bad!" His eyes got as big as saucers as he looked up at me. His mouth was open as wide as the Grand Canyon, but he said nothing. Instead, he quickly turned around, jumped in his car, and drove away. I admit I chuckled to myself. This trip had been worth it after all, and hopefully, that kid learned a valuable lesson.

Why do I tell you this story? Because it's time for some of us to stand up! I didn't look dangerous to the kid when I was sitting down. He was used to intimidating people and wasn't expecting me to actually stand up to him. When I did, he quickly realized he was outmatched. I called his bluff. This is how the devil works. First Peter 5:8 tells us he goes about *like a roaring lion, seeking whom he may devour.* The roar of the lion is meant to strike fear in the heart of its prey. Satan's desire is to intimidate us into fear and submission. But as a born-again, redeemed child of God, he isn't nearly as tough as he wants you to believe. He has zero power over you unless you give it to him.

SATAN IS NO "WANNABE"

Satan is no wannabe, and that is the reason Peter urges us in First Peter 5:8 to *"be sober, be vigilant."* Satan is a very dangerous adversary who will hit you hard if you drop your guard. But Satan knows the truth—you have been set free by the blood of Jesus. You are no longer under Satan's authority and no longer under sin's penalty, which means you are no longer under Satan's slavery. You are now in a different Kingdom, and you have a different King!

> Satan doesn't want you to discover your true identity or your power and authority in Christ.

As a child of God, you carry power and authority—Kingdom authority! Satan doesn't want you to ever discover your true identity in Christ or your power and authority as a Kingdom warrior. He knows you're no threat as long as you're sitting down.

When you stand up in the power of our risen Christ, you become dangerous. That's why four times in Ephesians 6:10-17, the apostle Paul tells us to *"stand"* or *"withstand."* It's time to take a stand. I wrote this book to help you do just that. STAND against the wiles and schemes of the devil. We are to:

- STAND against the fiery darts of the wicked one.
- WITHSTAND in the evil day.
- STAND in the whole armor of God.

If you are going to take a stand, you better be sure you are knowledgeable of who or what you are standing against. You don't want any surprises like that kid in the parking lot experienced. We understand there are fallen angels that rebelled with Satan. We know from the previous section why the apostle Paul referred to them as the rulers of the darkness of this age and spiritual hosts of wickedness in the heavenly places. In Ephesians 6:12, Paul gets very specific about these fallen angels:

> *For we do not wrestle against flesh and blood, but against principalities, against powers....*

The Bible is a self-interpreting book. By comparing Scripture with Scripture, you can discern what God is saying. Paul is teaching us that the angelic realm is ordered through a chain of command. Everything God does is through a chain of command or a hierarchy of authority. God knows that where there is no authority, there is anarchy. Whether human civilizations or such God-ordained institutions as the Church or the family, God works through a structure of authority because He knows otherwise it will be anarchy.

What is anarchy? It's war. It's chaos. It's confusion. Our entire society is in a time of moral anarchy. The average American family is in a state of anarchy. For some, even our lives personally are in a state of anarchy. It is insanity, chaos, and confusion—and it is because we have failed to submit to God's structure of authority. We've usurped God's authority, and our growing epidemic of addiction, depression, divorce, suicide, STDs, broken hearts, and broken lives are what we have to show for it. We have sowed to the wind, and we are reaping the whirlwind (Hosea 8:7).

Satan was the first usurper of God's authority when he said in Isaiah 14:13, *"I will ascend into heaven, I will exalt my throne above the stars of God....*" God had given him the second chair, but he wanted the first chair. He wanted to sit in God's chair, and he sowed rebellion within the angelic ranks.

ANGELIC CHAIN OF COMMAND

God ordered the angelic realm in a chain of command. That chain of command still stands to this day. If you are ready to take your stand, you need to understand the chain of command. To stand in victory against these demonic principalities and powers, it's crucial that you understand the command structure and where you, as a child of God, stand in that chain of command.

To take your stand, you need to understand the chain of command.

Principalities and powers appear to be two of the ranks among the angels, specifically the fallen angels. Compare what Paul writes in Ephesians 6:12 with what he writes in Colossians 1:16. It says, *"For by Him all things were created that are in heaven and that are on earth, visible and invisible, whether thrones or dominions or principalities or powers...."* God is illustrating through the pen of the apostle Paul the different ranks among the angels—both God's and Satan's—and their descending hierarchy of power and authority: thrones, dominions, principalities, and powers.

Long before Lucifer rebelled against God, taking one-third of the angels with him according to Revelation 12:4, God ordered the angelic realm through a chain of command, a structure of authority. In the same way the U.S. military has a command structure, Satan's demonic army and God's angelic army also have a command structure.

There are different ranks among the angels, both God's and Satan's. Paul is describing a hierarchy of power—descending powers of authority that Paul identifies as thrones, dominions, principalities, and powers.

Thrones and dominions are not mentioned in Ephesians 6:12 when Paul illustrates the demonic powers that we wrestle against. A comparison of Colossians 1:16 and Ephesians 6:12 reveals the two highest ranks of angels—thrones and dominions—did not rebel with Satan but rather sided with God.

Lucifer was a type of archangel of God, specifically called the *"anointed cherub"* in Ezekiel 28:14. That word "anointed" is the same Hebrew word as "messiah." The word "messiah" means "anointed one," and Satan was the messianic cherub before he rebelled. Don't confuse that title as making him equal to Jesus the Messiah! He has never been Jesus' equal—Jesus is deity, the second Person of the Trinity.

Unlike Jesus, who is eternal and everlasting, Satan had a beginning. He was created by God and *"perfect"* in all his ways *"from the day* [he was] *created, till iniquity was found in* [him]" (Ezekiel 28:15). God did not create Satan as evil; rather, He created him in perfection as the "anointed cherub." That title carries power and authority. It tells us that before his rebellion, Satan was the highest rank and authority of all the angels and the leader of the entire angelic host.

Satan still has the highest rank among the angels, both good and evil, which is why Jude 9 says, *"Yet Michael the archangel...when he disputed* [Satan] *about the body of Moses, dared not bring against him a reviling accusation, but said, 'The Lord rebuke you!'"* It appears that Michael, the archangel of God, is today the most powerful and highest-ranking member of the heavenly host. Yet Michael understood the chain of command. He knew he was not an angel with the same degree of power or authority as Satan.

Michael, a very powerful angel, yet weaker than Satan in power and authority, was taking a stand against him. Michael understood the Lord's name carried more power and more authority than any other name in the universe. That's why Paul begins his dissertation on spiritual warfare in Ephesians 6:10 saying, *"Be strong in the Lord and in the power of His might."* Michael was doing just that by invoking the Lord's name.

Just as Michael took his stand against the enemy, we must also. Satan is our mortal enemy and we are his. Two kingdoms are colliding, and the outcome has never been in doubt. But until the High King of Heaven returns to the earth, the battle will rage and it is real. The rebellion that began in the heavenlies continues today. As Satan went through the ranks of the angels, he was dividing and sowing dissension, trying to persuade the angels to rebel against God with him.

The two highest ranks—thrones and dominions—sided with God, which is why Paul doesn't mention them in Ephesians 6:12. The lower ranks—principalities and powers—sided with Satan. Eventually, he led one-third of them away (Revelation 12:4) into what we now know through the pen of the apostle Paul in Ephesians 6:12 are the fallen, demonic angels who at one time were God's angels. Paul said they were *"spiritual hosts of wickedness in the heavenly places."* That does not mean there is wickedness in heaven, at least not in the terms we normally think about heaven. Heaven is a holy, sinless place of perfection. Yet Paul says spiritual wickedness in the heavenly places.

THREE HEAVENS

There are three heavens described in Scripture. Genesis 1:1 records, *"In the beginning God created the heavens and the earth."* God created *"heavens,"* plural, not one heaven. The apostle Paul says in Second Corinthians 12:2 that he had been *"caught up to the third heaven,"* the dwelling place of God. Psalm 148 tells us about the three heavens. The third heaven is the dwelling place of God, the second heaven is what we commonly call outer space, and the first heaven is the earth and its atmosphere. Paul says spiritual wickedness in the heavenly places referring to the second heaven.

Satan currently rules from the second heaven, having been cast out of the third heaven. He is not in hell. He will be some day but not yet. In fact, he is going to avoid it as long as he can. Ephesians 2:2 calls him the *"prince of the power of the air,"* because he plans his assault upon the earth from the heavenlies. The Bible tells us in Daniel 10, there is warfare taking place right now in the heavenlies between the angels of God and the angels of Satan.

CHAPTER 4

PRINCIPALITIES
AND POWERS

For we do not wrestle against flesh and blood, but against principalities, against powers, against the rulers of the darkness of this age, against spiritual hosts of wickedness in the heavenly places (Ephesians 6:12).

In order to help you understand what Paul is talking about when he writes *"principalities and powers,"* think of it in terms of a municipality—a city or town. When I was a member of the KCPD, I had delegated authority given to me by the municipality of Kansas City, Missouri. Outside the city limits of my municipality, I had no authority. I was just a regular guy. But inside the specific region or piece of real estate where I had been assigned, I had powers others didn't have. Within my municipality, I had delegated authority. God has ordered the angelic realm in the same way by assigning delegated authority to certain angels to oversee certain regions of the world.

A principality refers to an entire country or region geographically. God has appointed angels to rule over and protect certain nations. Daniel 10 refers to Michael the archangel as a prince. He is the godly principality over the nation of Israel. Daniel 12:1 tells us that he is the protector and guardian angel over Israel.

Just as God has delegated authority to some of His angels, Satan has delegated authority to some of his fallen angels as well. Daniel 10:13 tells us there is a demonic prince called the prince of the kingdom of Persia, and Daniel 10:20 says there was a demonic prince over Greece. Satan had assigned a demonic prince to reign over the principalities of Persia and Greece as those world kingdoms were emerging. We learn in Daniel 10 that a full two hundred years before the Greek Empire emerged, Satan was already preparing a demonic being to reign over that empire.

The apostle Paul tells us we are wrestling against these principalities that are the demonic princes Satan has assigned to lord over specific regions of the world, specific kingdoms, and countries. We are at war with them, and they are at war with us. Satan makes these strategic assignments for one reason. We are a threat to him and his desire to establish his own kingdom in opposition to God's Kingdom.

Here's the point: Any time you are a threat to Satan, he will oppose whatever God is doing and wherever God is going.

If you believe the Bible and you understand what Paul is saying in Ephesians 6, it would be foolish to think Satan hasn't noticed the advances of the Church. This is spiritual warfare in its most fundamental form.

While principalities refer to powerful demonic beings who lord over specific regions or nations, powers represent lower-ranking demons assigned to specific cities, communities, people, or entities within a given geographic region or principality. Consequently, Satan assigns demonic powers for the purpose of sowing dissension and division, discord and discouragement, for no other reason than to divert, distract, or completely destroy the work of God, the people of God, the Church of God, and the plan of God because we are taking ground for God.

The primary principle of warfare: The army that takes the most ground wins.

Possessing enemy-held territory—taking real estate—is the nature of any war. Whether it's locally or globally, across this nation or around the world, every time someone comes to faith in Jesus Christ and is born again, that person is redeemed from Satan's slavery, and ground is taken from the enemy. Born-again believers now have Christ's liberty, and ground has been taken that was once enemy-held territory.

This is the reality and the reason Satan wars against us. It is why he tries so hard to oppose us at every turn. We would be naive to not believe that in this warfare he assigns demonic powers to our churches to hinder, discourage, stop, tempt, divide, and destroy God's people. I learned long ago that not everybody who walks through the doors of the church has been sent by God. Sometimes they've been sent by the devil.

> Most people are in a battle in which they are completely unaware.

Some people are prisoners unaware. I don't presume to know if they realize they are on a mission from Satan. Most people are participants in a battle in which they are completely unaware. They are oblivious to the fact that they are Satan's puppets, and he is using them and pulling their strings. These people have never really been redeemed; consequently, they are easily manipulated. They sow discord and division, and their primary objective is to divide and conquer. Satan's method is no different from any military operation.

I'm convinced Satan has assigned specific demonic beings to me in order to tempt, try, hinder, discourage, and stop me. Why? Because I'm a threat to the enemy and so are you! If you are living in such a way to bring glory to God, he has assigned demonic powers to you as well.

In Acts 19, the apostle Paul had been to Ephesus where they were experiencing a great move of God. The people of Ephesus were turning from their pagan gods to the true and living God.

People were watching Paul cast out demons, heal the sick, and do other supernatural things in the name of Jesus. But there are always some wannabes. These were people who didn't really know Jesus— they just wanted the power of Jesus. They thought they had stumbled onto a new incantation; some hocus pocus they could use to do all the cool things the apostle Paul was doing. They found a man who was demon possessed, and they told the demon to come out in Jesus' name. The demon talked back and said, *"Jesus I know, and Paul I know; but who are you?"* (Acts 19:15). In other words, I know of Jesus and I've heard of Paul, but I don't know who I'm talking to here.

Here's the point: If you are a threat to the enemy, your name is known in heaven and also in hell.

Jesus was known in hell; Paul was known in hell. These wannabes weren't known in hell because they weren't a real threat to the enemy. If you are a threat to the enemy, he will be relentless in coming at you to stop you in your tracks. Don't let that scare you. You have nothing to fear because Satan is no longer your king. You are no longer under his authority as a born-again believer, and together we are advancing God's Kingdom with every soul He saves.

Every person who comes to Christ advances God's Kingdom.

Every time another person comes to Christ, we're advancing God's Kingdom. At the same time, Satan is trying to advance his with every man, woman, and child he takes captive. It's spiritual warfare between two opposing armies, two opposing kings, and two opposing kingdoms. The good news is that you're on the side of God—you're on the winning side.

Even though Satan has angels warring against you, God has angels warring for you. There is a host of angelic bodyguards surrounding my church and my house, protecting me, my family, and my congregation. Nothing can happen to me that does not pass through God's absolute sovereignty. I am under Jesus' authority, and you are as well as a child of God.

You never go into warfare without getting dressed for battle by putting on your armor, *"that you may be able to stand against the wiles* [or the schemes] *of the devil."* This means Satan and his army of demonic beings plan, plot, strategize, and scheme against us.

Satan is not infinite like God. He is a finite creature like you and me, but he is far wiser and far more powerful. Because he's not infinite in nature, he's not omnipotent (all powerful); he's not omniscient (all knowing); he's not omnipresent (everywhere). Unlike God, he's extremely wise, but he's not all wise; although he's extremely powerful, he's not all powerful. Unlike God, he can't be everywhere at once, which is why he has an army of fallen angels warring for him and gathering intelligence information to use against us.

A satanic or spiritual attack is a purposeful, well-planned assault by the enemy. He might attack us spiritually, emotionally, mentally, physically, financially, or relationally; but as a blood-bought child of the living God, you are under God's authority. All of Satan's assaults must pass through God's sovereignty. Satan has to stop where God says stop. He cannot do anything he wants because he does not have ultimate authority over you. Only God has authority over you.

What Satan can do, however, is manipulate people, circumstances, and situations in such a way as to tempt, discourage, afflict, or destroy you. Remember, Jesus told us in John 10:10 that Satan's ultimate goal is to steal, kill, and destroy. He wants to separate you from God and ultimately destroy your life. He wants to overcome us, but the Bible teaches we can overcome him. This is warfare. One will win, one will lose.

LEARNING HOW TO TAKE YOUR STAND

And they overcame him [Satan] *by the blood of the Lamb and by the word of their testimony, and they did not love their lives to the death* (Revelation 12:11).

In Revelation 12:11, God gives us three keys to successfully stand against the enemy: 1) Your spiritual position, 2) Your mouth's confession, and 3) Your life's submission.

The context of this verse speaks of the tribulation saints who will be mercilessly persecuted by the devil during the great tribulation shortly before Christ returns to establish His earthly Kingdom. The same keys to their victory in *the* tribulation are the same keys to victory in *our* tribulation.

As any soldier knows, a fundamental principle of warfare is simply this—whoever has the high ground wins. All historic battles have been fought over the high ground because that is the greatest position of advantage in warfare. As Christians, we don't have to take the high ground because we already *have* it! Jesus took it for us 2,000 years ago when He walked up the hill of Calvary. He fought, bled, and died, but He came out of that tomb alive. He's the Victor, and that means you don't have to live like a victim. We are not fighting for victory. We *have* victory already!

Here's the point: It's not up to us to take any ground—Jesus has taken it for us. It's not up to us to advance against the enemy—Jesus already did. He is our high ground, our high tower, our fortified position.

You are not fighting for victory. You are fighting from a place of victory: *"And they overcame him by the blood of the Lamb..."* (Revelation 12:11).

The blood of Jesus is your victory. He has redeemed you by His blood from sin's penalty and Satan's tyranny. You are no longer under condemnation, and Satan can bring no accusation. Your victory is secured already by the blood of Calvary. Your spiritual position is your elevated and fortified position "in Christ." When you belong to the Victor, you don't have to live defeated, you can live dynamically. You don't have to live vanquished, you can live victoriously.

> *Blessed be the Lord my Rock, who trains my hands for war, and my fingers for battle...my fortress, my high tower...my shield...* (Psalm 144:1-2).

> *The Lord is my rock and my fortress and my deliverer; my God, my strength, in whom I will trust; my shield and the horn of my salvation, my stronghold* (Psalm 18:2).

Satan no longer has authority over you; you have authority over him according to Luke 10:19. Christ has given us victory from sin's penalty, and His blood has given us victory from sin's power. He has overcome Satan's slavery and Satan's tyranny. No longer are we in captivity; the blood of Jesus has overcome the bondage of sin. Because of the blood, we have an elevated, fortified position of victory, power, liberty, and authority.

> *Put on the whole armor of God, that you may be able to stand against the wiles of the devil....Therefore take up the whole armor of God, that you may be able to withstand in the evil day, and having done all, to stand. Stand therefore...* (Ephesians 6:11, 13-14).

Four times in three verses Paul tells us to "stand." Paul is simply saying to stand on the finished work of Jesus Christ and His shed blood on Calvary. That is the high ground!

Romans 10:13 says, *"Whoever calls on the name of the Lord shall be saved."* When you call on the name of Jesus, your sins are under the blood of the Lamb—100 percent of them. If even one sin was left uncovered by the blood, that one sin would be enough to keep you out of heaven because it's a place of perfection. But when you call upon Jesus, you are 100 percent forgiven of sin's penalty and 100 percent free from sin's power. That includes the "big" ones, all the things you would love to forget about, and the "little" ones you've already forgotten. In fact, God has already forgiven things you haven't even done yet. Because you are in Christ, positionally, everything you have ever done that was evil and everything you are ever going to do that is evil is under the blood—every sin—past, present, and future.

> *Not by works of righteousness which we have done, but according to His mercy He saved us...* (Titus 3:5).

You can't lose your salvation because you didn't work for it. It was Christ and Christ alone who did all the work. His work cannot be undone by your work or Satan's work, because His work is greater. If you have to stand on what you've done, you are in trouble. Paul says stand on what Christ has done—the finished work of the Lamb.

CHAPTER 5

THE ACCUSER

Then I heard a loud voice saying in heaven, "Now salvation, and strength, and the kingdom of our God, and the power of His Christ have come, for the accuser of our brethren [brothers and sisters in Christ], *who accused them before our God day and night, has been cast down* (Revelation 12:10).

I hope there has been a time in your life when you have called on the name of Jesus and your sins were forgiven. But has there ever been a time in your life after you were saved when you woke up one morning and Satan was sitting on the end of your bed accusing you of being guilty, undeserving, unworthy, and digging up everything you ever did?

I'm talking about those nagging accusations in your ear about those things you have repented of that are under the blood. "Don't you remember what you did when you were 16, 17, or 18? Don't you remember what you did last week, last month, and last year? Don't you remember what you did yesterday? How can you say you are a Christian? How can you say that you are forgiven? You are not good enough to be a Christian. There's no way you can be a child of God."

He begins digging up everything you ever did, and he tries to convince you that your sins cannot possibly be forgiven. He's trying to convince you that you're still in slavery and captivity and you're not really in victory and liberty. He does that because as Revelation 12:10 tells us, he's the accuser of our brethren. He's trying to convince you to give up the high ground.

In Hebrew, his name is Satan; in the Greek, he is the devil. They both mean the same thing: accuser. His nature is one of an accuser, and he wants to accuse, prosecute, and destroy you. The Bible teaches in Revelation 12:10 that Satan comes before God in the great tribunal room of heaven, as *"the accuser of our brethren…day and night."* Like a prosecuting attorney, he comes before God peering into the third heaven from the second heaven, accusing us of sin. He looks at God and says, "Did You see what Phil just did? Phil can't be a son of God, he just sinned. Phil can't be forgiven. Do You really think Phil loves You? Phil doesn't love You. Look at what he just did."

Here's the point: We have an Advocate with the Father, the great Judge in heaven, and His name is Jesus, Jesus Christ the Righteous.

The Bible says in First John 2:1 that *"we have an Advocate with the Father, Jesus Christ the righteous."* As the prosecutor, the devil comes before God accusing us. Jesus, our Advocate, stands up from His throne and walks over before the Father and He intercedes for us as our High Priest (Hebrews 8:1). He gets in between Satan and the Father and He says, "Hang on there, devil. I have something to say."

He comes before God as the great Judge, and He shows the Father the nail prints in His hands. He looks at the Father and says, "I bled for that sin, I died for that sin, and I'm their Advocate. I'm the One who laid down my life for that sin. Phil is indeed a son of God. He is the redeemed of God, and he is under the blood of the Lamb of God." The Father looks at the devil and says, "I find him innocent."

The righteousness of Christ is upon me— God put my sin upon His Son.

God has put the righteousness of Christ upon me, and He put my sin upon His Son (2 Corinthians 5:21). He bore my sin in my place so that now when He looks at me, God no longer sees my sin; He simply sees the righteousness of the Son. Satan cannot accuse us before God, so he comes and accuses us to make us feel unworthy and undeserving. He wants us to feel like hypocrites.

I'm not qualified to be a Christian much less a pastor because of my so-called righteous works. Isaiah 64:6 says our righteousness compared to the righteousness of God is as *"filthy rags."* I'm qualified for one reason—because of Christ's work. It's not by my righteousness but rather Christ's righteousness. There have been times when I have not felt worthy of standing before my congregation on a Sunday morning. The devil wants to disarm me by reminding me of my own issues so he can lure me down from the high ground.

Regardless of what accusations Satan brings against you, remember you are worthy to serve God for one reason—the blood of the Lamb. He wants you to feel unworthy to be a child of God, unworthy to be redeemed of God. "Well, I don't deserve forgiveness." Of course you don't, that's why it's called grace. If you deserved it, you wouldn't need it. Satan wants you to walk in guilt instead of grace so he can keep you in slavery instead of victory and take back the high ground in your life spiritually. He wants to take you to a place of captivity instead of living what Jesus calls abundant life.

> *They overcame him by the blood of the Lamb and by the word of their testimony* (Revelation 12:11).

In the battle of the ages, you can't pick and choose your weapons. According to Ephesians 6:13, you are not only to stand on the finished *work* of the Son of God, you are to stand on the *truth* of the Word of God. You overcome with the blood of the Lamb by standing on the finished work of the Son of God—*and* you must also overcome by the Word of your testimony. That is your verbal witness of God's Word.

You stand against the enemy first by your spiritual position and next by your mouth's confession. Two of the greatest weapons you have in your arsenal are praise and proclamation. When you choose to praise God in the face of tribulation and speak the promises of God into your situation, you are overcoming everything Satan tries to bring against you in his attempt to gain back the high ground in your life.

> The Word of God is the most powerful weapon in the universe.

The Word of God is the most powerful weapon in the universe. It was the Word of God that spoke light into the darkness, creation out of nothingness, and brought the Son of God back from the dead. It is the Word of God—the sword of the Spirit—that Satan fears above all. He will do anything to keep you from engaging him in combat with it because the sword of the Spirit is the one weapon that can send him running.

All he has are lies to lure us down off the high ground. You defend the high ground by standing on the Truth. But you can't just quote the Word of God repeatedly like it has some magical power against the enemy.

Here's the point: It does no good just to know and declare what God says if you do not *believe* what God says and won't *do* what God says.

You appropriate the promises of God practically by believing what God has said is your ultimate reality. People can say what they think, but they do what they believe. The word of your testimony is in your belief and obedience to the Word of God. Satan may be whispering in your ear and you don't feel victorious, but God has already said you are. Victory in your life doesn't depend on your circumstances or situation—it depends on you standing on the blood of the Lamb.

"Well, I don't feel like I'm worthy." God says you are worthy.

"But I don't feel victorious." God says you have victory already.

You learn to trust what God has said, regardless of what you feel. That is how you appropriate the promises of God. It is the same way you were saved and overcame sin's penalty. You did it by putting your faith in what God said in Ephesians 2:8, *"For by grace you have been saved through faith...."* You appropriated both forgiveness from sin and all the promises of God by saying, "I will believe what God has said regardless of what I see. I will believe the facts of God's Word regardless of what I feel." That's how you begin overcoming by the blood of the Lamb, speaking forth the word of your testimony, which is the Word of God. So take your stand!

Learn to trust what God has said, regardless of what you feel.

Learn to make a verbal confession, proclamation, and declaration of God's Word and God's promises in the face of every situation, trial, temptation, and tribulation. You combat the lies of the enemy with the truth of God's Word! Satan's lies are always how he attempts to lure you down from the high ground.

Finally, these tribulation saints are going to lay down their lives literally according to Revelation 12:11, *"They did not love their lives to the death."* They're going to die, but in dying, they overcome. Jesus said in Mark 8:35, *"Whoever desires to save his life will lose it, but whoever loses his life for My sake and the gospel's will save it."*

It's the great paradox of the Christian life... to live, you have to die. To go up, you have to go down.

As you die to self, you die to sin; you overcome Satan, and you live for the Savior. This is the key to victory over the enemy. In order to live the life of victory God wants you to live, you must first let go of the life you have. This is the reason so many are still struggling against temptation and tribulation and being overcome so easily by Satan. They are still hanging on and holding on instead of giving up and giving in.

As long as you are hanging on to your life, Satan will hang on to you. The moment you let go of your life, Satan has no choice but to let go too. Now somebody else is hanging on to you—your Lord and Savior Jesus Christ. If you will lay your life down, God will pick it up.

You stand against the enemy by your spiritual position, your mouth's confession, and finally your life's submission. The apostle Paul wrote in First Corinthians 15:31, *"I die daily."* He was confessing to God that his life was not his own. He had given it completely to Him.

The key to victory is surrendering all rights to your life and giving all rights to the Lord Jesus Christ every moment of every day. How do you stand against the devil? You do it by submitting completely to God. *"Therefore submit to God. Resist the devil and he will flee from you"* (James 4:7). How do you get the devil to flee from you? By submitting to God.

> Here is the paradox: You stand up by bowing down. That's how you take your stand and take back stolen ground!

Every soldier in combat knows the most dangerous adversary is the one who's not afraid to die. This is what made the Japanese such a difficult enemy in WWII. Kamikaze pilots would nose-dive their planes into Allied aircraft carriers and use their planes as missiles, thinking nothing of their own lives. Their infantry would choose to fight to the death, even when they knew they couldn't actually win, rather than to surrender and be taken alive. Defeating an enemy that has already given up their life is next to impossible—they have nothing left to lose.

This is our ultimate victory. By laying down our lives, we overcome our enemy because there is nothing he can do to us or take from us that we haven't already given away to Jesus. What are you worried about losing? Your finances? Your future? Your family? Your health? Your wealth?

Here's the point: You first must be overcome by Christ before you can overcome Satan. And you will never successfully stand against Satan until you have bowed before your Savior.

You can't lose what you've already given to God—it all belongs to Him. Take a moment to think about what you may be holding on to and give it all to God. Satan can't take anything from you—including life itself.

For to me, to live is Christ, and to die is gain (Philippians 1:21).

...they did not love their lives to the death (Revelation 12:11).

If you will die to self, you will die to sin, and you will then live for the Savior and overcome Satan. I die daily, sometimes moment by moment, in the face of temptation. I'm dead, and I cannot sin unless I choose to live. This is what it means to live in victory.

PART III

ANCHOR YOUR LIFE TO THE TRUTH

Finally, my brethren, be strong in the Lord and in the power of His might. Put on the whole armor of God, that you may be able to stand against the wiles of the devil. For we do not wrestle against flesh and blood, but against principalities, against powers, against the rulers of the darkness of this age, against spiritual hosts of wickedness in the heavenly places. Therefore take up the whole armor of God, that you may be able to withstand in the evil day, and having done all, to stand. Stand therefore, having girded your waist with truth, having put on the breastplate of righteousness, and having shod your feet with the preparation of the gospel of peace; above all, taking the shield of faith with which you will be able to quench all the fiery darts of the wicked one. And take the helmet of salvation, and the sword of the Spirit, which is the word of God (Ephesians 6:10-17).

How do you get dressed in the morning? I'll tell you how I get dressed in the morning. It entirely depends on what I'm planning to do that day. As I write this, I am currently wearing workout shorts, an old oversized T-shirt, and no shoes or socks, just bare feet. It's a Monday morning, and I don't plan on seeing anybody for most of the day. I'm dressed for comfort, not fashion. I'm not dressed to impress.

Yesterday at this time, I had on a nice shirt, khaki-colored jeans, and dress shoes. Why the different attire? Yesterday I was preaching to my congregation. This morning I'm drinking a cup of coffee in my recliner. In a couple of hours, I'll go down to my basement and work out with my son. It's bench-press day. The shorts I'm wearing and the oversized T-shirt will be perfect when I work up a sweat.

After that, I'll change clothes. I need to mow my lawn. I'll take off the workout shorts and put on an old pair of jean shorts. I'll probably wear the same oversized T-shirt I've already perspired in. I'll change into jean shorts because my kids tell me jean shorts are "out" and no longer "in." The shorts I bought ten years ago and once considered fashionable will now suffice for work. By the time you read this, they will probably be back in style. But for now, they are perfect for getting dirty. I'll put flip-flops on my feet before climbing onto my zero-turn riding mower.

Then I'll come in, clean up, and put on an entirely different set of clothes. My son just had his 21st birthday, and his mother and I are taking him out tonight for dinner to celebrate. We're splurging on a very nice restaurant in one of the upscale areas of Kansas City. Instead of my workout shorts or my goofy jean shorts, I'll put on a pair of designer jeans. Instead of the flip-flops or tennis shoes I had on earlier, I'll put on a really nice pair of dress shoes and one of my fitted dress shirts. I'll dress for the occasion and dress for fashion. When I walk into that restaurant, I'll look like I didn't just stumble in off the street. I will be wearing a completely different set of clothes that reflect my plans. Can you imagine if I showed up to that upscale restaurant still wearing my flip flops and dirty jean shorts? I'm afraid they might call the police!

Tomorrow morning I'm preaching a funeral for one of the precious members of our church who passed into heaven last week. I'll put on one of my least favorite outfits—my black suit—complete with white shirt and tie. How much sense would it make for me to mow my lawn today while wearing my black suit? Or to show up tomorrow to the funeral wearing my flip-flops and dirty jean shorts? Everyone dresses for the day based on their plans. No one haphazardly puts on whatever they happen to be wearing. Most people put at least a little thought into it.

DRESS FOR BATTLE

This is why the apostle Paul tells us to dress for battle every day—not for a picnic or a formal dinner—but for battle. The clothes you wear are based on the anticipated activity for the day. Sadly, most Christians put almost no thought into how they dress spiritually. They make no preparations for the battle with the unseen enemy they will engage in that day. It's a battle that begins the moment you crawl out of bed and your feet hit the floor.

If we take Ephesians 6:10-17 seriously and anticipate the battle that is coming with our unseen enemy every day, we will put on the whole armor of God as part of our morning routine. God has given us all we need to live in victory daily against all the power of the adversary, and the apostle Paul is teaching the art of spiritual warfare and how to dress for battle daily.

We live in a world that is truly at war, and we're part of that warfare. Since Cain slew his brother Abel in the book of Genesis, the history of humanity has been awash with bloodshed, war, and violence. From the very moment Adam sinned, sending creation into chaos and ruining the perfection of God's creation, it has been spinning out of control. Sin ruined what God had done and the perfection from which it came. The chaos of our world is simply a reflection of the warfare taking place in the spiritual world.

We are part of a world at war.

Remember, Satan is at war with God; therefore, he is at war with the people of God. This is why Paul instructs us in verse 13 to *"take up the whole armor of God, that you may be able to withstand* [the devil] *in the evil day."* The evil day is any day that Satan attempts to afflict us, torment us, tempt us in some way, or bring tribulation upon us. As the redeemed of God and the children of God, we are part of the Kingdom of God. Satan wants to stop us because this is a battle of opposing kings and opposing kingdoms.

As the people of God, we are advancing the Kingdom of God, but as we advance God's Kingdom, Satan wants to advance his. Each day when you wake up, you face another battle. We need to dress for battle and prepare to withstand in the evil day. When Paul says, *"the evil day,"* he's not talking about one specific day, but that we live in this evil world where every day is an evil day. Some days are more evil than others. Some days the battles are more intense than others. Some days the affliction is a little hotter than the one before—but every single day is the evil day Paul is talking about in this verse.

Paul is telling you to stand against all the wiles of the devil—to stand against his affliction, his tribulation, his torments, his trials. Whatever he brings against you, God has given you everything you need to stand against all the power of the enemy. Understand that it takes supernatural weapons to fight a supernatural enemy. You have spiritual weapons and armor so you can stand against all the power of the adversary.

You don't fight spiritual warfare with physical weapons. It is as futile to fight Satan with human intellect, reasoning, philosophy, or willpower as it would be with grenade launchers or assault rifles. This is why Paul says, *"Be strong in the Lord and in the power of His might."*

There is only one Power in the universe that is more powerful than Satan's, and that is the absolute power and authority of Jesus Christ. In Ephesians 6, Paul instructs us how to put on the armor of God so you can stand. Once you know how the enemy operates, you can learn how to dress for battle, one piece of armor at a time. Before you think about putting on the armor, I want you to understand something remarkable—Christ is your armor.

CHRIST IS YOUR ARMOR

Christ is the embodiment and the essence of every piece of armor Paul describes. This is why over and over again in the New Testament we're told to put on the Lord Jesus Christ. Romans 13:14 says, *"Put on the Lord Jesus Christ...."* He is our shield of faith, He is the helmet of salvation, He is the belt of truth, and He is the sword of the Spirit.

Isaiah 59:17-18 is a messianic prophecy that directly deals with the person of Jesus Christ:

> *For He* [Jesus] *put on righteousness as a breastplate, and a helmet of salvation on His head; He put on the garments of vengeance for clothing...according to their deeds, accordingly He will repay, fury to His adversaries, recompense to His enemies...."*

This passage is describing Jesus Christ, a Messiah warrior; He is the warrior King, and He is mighty in battle. This might be at least one of the Old Testament passages Paul had in mind as he penned the New Testament revelation of Ephesians 6:10-17.

So much for the wimpy little pacifist Jesus of the modern church age. Rather, He is the warrior King, and He is dressed for battle. Jesus is the One Joshua saw as he stared up at the walls of Jericho. It seemed as impenetrable and unwinnable as the Jerichos you may be facing in your own life. It seemed impenetrable to Joshua, but then he saw the pre-incarnate Jesus Christ in full battle dress who said He was the *"Commander of the army of the Lord"* who went before them into battle (Joshua 5:14). He had His sword out, ready to go. The One who went before Joshua is the same One who went before you 2,000 years ago on the cross of Calvary. He has won the day, and He is the same One who can win every day. All you have to do is stand.

Many people see Jesus only as a suffering servant hanging helplessly on the cross. He is indeed the Lamb of God, but He is also the Lion of the tribe of Judah. As the Lamb, He came to suffer, but as the Lion, He is our Warrior. Remember, He is no longer on the cross, nor is He in the tomb! Yet we so often act like Jesus is struggling for existence in the universe instead of remembering that He is alive and exercising power and authority as King of kings and Lord of lords! In a world of many gods, He has no equal.

Jesus says in Matthew 16:18, *"...on this rock I will build My church, and the gates of Hades shall not prevail against it."* He has promised we will prevail and Satan will lose! We are on the winning side because we are on the side of the Lord Jesus Christ. In Revelation 1:18, He says, *"I am He who lives, and was dead, and behold, I am alive forevermore...."* He came out of the grave and has forever won the day!

Satan knows he is a defeated adversary. He knows Jesus has won the victory, so he uses a common military tactic: diversion. On D-Day, June 6, 1944, part of the reason the Allied invasion of Nazi-controlled France succeeded is because General Dwight Eisenhower, commander of all Allied forces, sent a large number of troops in motion to the north just a few days before. He was creating a diversion. The Allies wanted Hitler and his army to think they were attacking from Norway, when all along the plan was to attack from France. So a few days before, they sent troops in motion to the north to make it look like the invasion was coming from Norway.

The Nazis took the bait and focused their troops on the wrong front. They shifted troops to the north, and the Allied troops struck from the south. They assaulted the beaches of Normandy, and by the time Hitler realized what was happening, it was too late.

Satan wants to do the very same thing to us. He creates a diversion so you will focus on the physical. That is why Paul says to remember, *"We do not wrestle against flesh and blood."* If you are trying to wage war focused only on what you can see, you are waging war focused on the wrong front. It's not physical; it's not flesh and blood.

The end is not in doubt, but the war still rages.

While the Allied victory on the beaches of Normandy on June 6, 1944, effectively assured a complete and unconditional surrender of the Nazi army, the war still raged on. Although the end was no longer in doubt once Allied forces successfully landed in France, the war in Europe would last for another year before Allied troops would finally reach Berlin.

That is a picture of our present situation as followers of Jesus. Two thousand years ago was D-Day spiritually. With the resurrection, Jesus has forever sealed our victory. The end is not in doubt. The Kingdom of light will prevail against the kingdom of darkness. Satan and his army of fallen angels will one day make a complete and unconditional surrender to the High King of the Universe.

> That at the name of Jesus every knee should bow, of those in heaven, and of those on earth, and of those under the earth, and that every tongue should confess that Jesus Christ is Lord, to the glory of God the Father (Philippians 2:10-11).

Yes, Satan and all his rebellious angels will one day bow before Jesus. But until that day, we must prepare to stand against the devil and dress for battle. The end is not in doubt, but the war still rages.

CHAPTER 6

THE BELT OF TRUTH

Stand therefore, having girded your waist with truth... (Ephesians 6:14).

I don't know about you, but the last thing I think about when I start putting together an outfit to wear is the belt. For me, the belt is kind of an afterthought—the last thing I put on. But when dressing for battle, Paul doesn't consider the belt an afterthought at all. It's not accidental that Paul begins describing our spiritual armor with the belt of truth. It's an essential part of the spiritual armor.

Modern warriors understand how important the belt is as they dress for battle. It carries the essential equipment they will need to succeed. In addition to my .40 caliber Smith and Wesson, my police belt carried extra magazines of ammunition, handcuffs, pepper spray, rubber gloves, a radio, as well as my PR-24 nightstick.

Modern warriors are no different from warriors in Jesus' day. They all understand the significance of the belt when they dress for battle. Such a seemingly insignificant part of their gear is actually an essential piece of equipment. When you dress for spiritual battle every day, you need to begin with the belt of truth. It's the first piece of equipment Paul describes in his description of our spiritual armor.

The first piece of armor a Roman soldier would have put on was the belt. Paul says, *"Stand therefore, having girded your waist with truth…."* As the apostle Paul wrote these words, he was a prisoner of Rome. Day after day he was being guarded by a Roman soldier. He would have been intimately familiar with the gear of a Roman soldier, and he had plenty of time to ponder and reflect on what he saw as the changing of the guard happened over and over, as one Roman soldier ended his shift and another was assigned to him.

As a Roman citizen, Paul would have seen Roman soldiers throughout the course of his life in full battle dress with a helmet, shield, and breastplate. As Paul was writing under the inspiration of the Holy Spirit, looking at this Roman soldier and his Roman armor, suddenly the Spirit started to move in him.

His mind flashed back to Isaiah 59:17: *"For He put on righteousness as a breastplate, and a helmet of salvation on His head…."* The eyes of his understanding were opened to see the reality of Jesus our warrior King. He is our Shield, our Sword, the Helmet of our Salvation, our Breastplate of Righteousness. Under the inspiration of the Holy Spirit, Paul made the connection that the Roman soldier's armor is a picture of our spiritual armor—the armor of God. He put pen to paper and wrote in Ephesians 6:13-14:

Therefore take up the whole armor of God, that you may be able to withstand in the evil day, and having done all, to stand. Stand therefore, having girded your waist with truth.

The number one thing Paul says we have to put on is the belt of truth. The King James Version of the Bible says it this way: *"Having your loins girt about with truth."* No one talks like that anymore in contemporary English. Loins are simply the strongest part of your body from which you can generate the most power. Anybody who knows anything about powerlifting knows you don't just bend over and pick something up, or you will blow out your back. Rather, you want to use your legs and hips.

A Roman soldier learned to fight with his hips because they were the strongest part of his body. Paul is saying when you have belted your waist with truth, you have never been stronger in all of your life. This piece of equipment wasn't a little two or three-inch belt, it was a four to six-inch-wide leather belt.

Consider the analogy Paul is making. There are several purposes for this belt. First of all, it was for support. Roman armor was heavy. The soldier would have worn this armor all day while standing for a long time or marching for long distances.

As a member of the Kansas City Police Department, I would often be on security detail as a member of the SWAT team. Sometimes we would stand in one place for hours, and the longer we stood, the more our backs began to ache. Roman soldiers had a very thick belt to give them back support. Paul calls our belt the belt of truth because when we have anchored our lives to the truth, it gives us back support. We need a strong backbone if we're going to stand against the enemy.

Not only that, but when a Roman soldier strapped on his belt, there were little tassels hanging down in front of his groin. They were weighted tassels meant to give him some protection from the low blows all men hate by softening the blow or deflecting it altogether. Think about it—whether you're a man or a woman, most of us have received a low blow in life from the devil. You know what I mean—a hit below the belt, a cheap shot. The devil is really good at cheap shots. Roman soldiers were equipped with a heavy leather belt with weighted tassels in front of the groin to protect them from those cheap shots, those hits below the belt—just as the belt of truth protects you from the devil's below-the-belt cheap shots.

The belt held the sword securely to the soldier's side so the sword was always in the ready position, and he was always ready for immediate action. The belt also held some other essentials like food and water. The Roman soldier's belt secured the breastplate in place. Without the belt, the breastplate would have bounced around any time the soldier ran into battle, galloped on a horse, or even moved very quickly. Without the belt holding the breastplate in place, the soldier would have been greatly hindered in battle.

Next, as the soldier prepared for battle, he would tie up his tunic. In Bible times, men didn't wear britches or pants, they wore tunics or skirts that came down to the knees, if not the ankles. Modern fatigues worn by today's soldiers were still centuries away. When Roman soldiers wanted to move quickly, they would secure their tunic to their belt to keep their legs from being encumbered. They would literally take their tunic, roll it up, and then tie it in their belt. Yes, they went into battle wearing what looked like a mini-skirt! That's what Paul had in his mind's eye as he wrote, *"having girded your waist with truth."* Paul means to tie up your tunic in your belt of truth and prepare for battle!

THE CENTER AND ANCHOR

This belt was the center and the anchor of all of the Roman soldier's equipment for battle. Everything else may look more important, but apart from the belt, nothing would have stayed in place or remained attached. In the very same way, Paul is teaching that biblical truth must be your center and your anchor. When you center your life on God's truth and you anchor your life to His truth, you put on the belt of truth.

We can know the Truth—the Truth is the Son of God, the Word of God.

In some ways, the United States is a nation adrift because our country has lost its truth anchor. So many people are floating aimlessly through life because they no longer have absolute truth as the center of their lives. There are a lot of people who debate whether we can know the truth. Jesus said in John 14:6, *"I am the way, the truth...."* Jesus is God's Word that *"became flesh and dwelt among us"* (John 1:14).

Here's the point: You cannot know truth apart from knowing a Person, and that Person is Jesus Christ. Jesus is more than true. He is Truth!

Not only is Jesus Christ truth, but Jesus said in John 17:17 as He prayed to the Father for us, *"Sanctify them by Your truth. Your word is truth."* Truth is found in the Living Word—Jesus—and the written Word—the Bible. We can know the truth because truth is in the Son of God, and the truth is in the Word of God. Like Jesus, the Bible is more than true. It is Truth!

Anything in this world that contradicts the Son of God or contradicts the Word of God is a lie—it is not truth. Until you thoroughly believe that for yourself, you have failed to put on the belt of truth, and you will be easily overcome by the enemy. Without the belt of truth anchoring your life, you will easily believe the enemy's arsenal of lies. When you believe the lies of the enemy, he will lead you into captivity.

It begins with that lie straight from the pit of hell that is completely taking over the mentality of our society that says, "There is no absolute truth; you can't know what the truth is. You define your truth for you, and I'll define my truth for me. There are no absolutes spiritually; there are no absolutes morally. You decide what's right for you, and I'll decide what's right for me." Not only is that kind of thinking unbiblical, it is illogical and completely hypocritical.

There is no human being on the face of the planet who really believes practically there are no absolutes. The moment somebody says, "There is no absolute truth," they have just made an absolute statement. Hypocrite!

Some people say there are no absolute laws morally or spiritually. Everyone can define their own truth. Yet take that mentality into the doctor's office when you need surgery. If I hear my surgeon say as I'm about to be taken into surgery, "Well, it doesn't really matter where I cut today. I think I'm going to cut over here, it's close enough"— I'm coming off that operating table! I want a doctor who has some absolute truth.

If you go to the pharmacist with a prescription to fill, and you hear the pharmacist say, "It doesn't really matter what pills you take. Here, take these pills, they're just as good as the other ones," you are not going to take those pills. You want a pharmacist who possesses absolute truth. Not just any pill will do. If I get on an airplane and I hear the pilot say, "It doesn't really matter which button I push today on this control panel, they all basically do the same thing," I'm getting off that plane! I need a pilot committed to some absolutes.

The reality is the world is controlled by absolutes. In the very same way there are absolute truths mathematically, there are absolute truths morally. Five plus five will always equal ten. Gravity is true whether you believe it or not. It doesn't change. It's irrevocable and irreversible. What goes up will come down. Whether or not you believe it doesn't change the fact that it's true.

The entire universe is controlled by absolutes, and everyone knows it. It's completely illogical to think there are absolute truths for everything except what is true spiritually and what is true morally. Yet people will argue against such absolutes morally and spiritually because it's really a matter of authority.

Truth is defined by the Living Word and by the written Word.

Like Lucifer before them, they want to usurp God's authority because to do otherwise would mean they would have to acknowledge He is God and they are not. In refusing to submit their lives to God, they make themselves a slave to the god of this age. Remember what Jesus said in John 8:32, *"You shall know the truth, and the truth shall make you free."* It is God who wants to set us free. It is Satan who wants to take us into captivity.

To live victoriously against the enemy you must begin by putting on the belt of truth. The Living Word is Christ; the written Word is the Bible. It's the Word of God that defines what is true and what is not. The Word of God is the absolute standard of reality. The Word of God rules, and it alone is our final authority. This is the mindset and confidence required to cinch up the belt of truth tightly lest you be taken captive by the enemy.

Why is this so important? Let me illustrate it this way. If you ask several people to tell you the time, you could get a variety of answers. Especially back in the days before everyone had cell phones and people actually wore watches to know the time. Now that everyone carries cell phones, watches are sold more for a fashion piece than a timepiece. Watches often don't agree on the correct time. One person's watch might be a minute fast while another might be two minutes slow.

We could argue all day about what time it is, but we don't have to because there's an absolute standard of time in Colorado. It's the government's atomic clock that sets the time for the entire nation. Cell phones always reflect the same time because they are all using the same standard of time.

TRUTH IS TIMELESS

In our current culture, people argue about what is true because they are all using their own standard when God Himself is the standard. People argue about things like the definition of marriage. The reason they can't all agree is because they are all using a different standard. Jesus, who is the Living Word, quoted from the Bible, the written Word, when asked a question about marriage. In doing so, He gave us God's absolute standard of marriage in Matthew 19:4-5, *"Have you not read that He who made them at the beginning 'made them male and female,' and said, 'For this reason a man shall leave his father and mother and be joined to his wife, and the two shall become one flesh'?"*

Here you have God's definition of marriage, and every other standard is false. It's not that the truth can't be known. It's that the world has decided it hates the truth. But denying the truth of God's standard of marriage no more changes the truth than denying the reality of gravity. Truth is timeless; it never ceases and it never changes. Every person you know can deny it, but it doesn't change the reality of the absolute truth of God.

People have argued for decades about when life begins in the womb. Once again we have an absolute standard of truth found in Psalm 139:13, 16:

> *For You formed my inward parts; you covered me in my mother's womb. ...Your eyes saw my substance, being yet unformed. And in Your book they all were written, the days fashioned for me, when as yet there were none of them.*

God saw you in your mother's womb as a human being even before you had a fully formed human body. He wrote about your days and recorded them in a book in heaven before you had lived any of them on earth. Once again, God has not hidden the truth from us.

The problem for us today is what Jesus said in John 3:19 (NIV), *"This is the verdict: Light has come into the world, but people loved darkness instead of light, because their deeds were evil."* Because of the rebellious hearts of the fallen sons of Adam and the fallen daughters of Eve, people naturally run to the darkness instead of the light. In so doing, they align themselves with the rulers of the darkness of this age. Instead of being free, they find themselves in slavery to the enemy.

As members of Adam's race, we were created in the image and likeness of God. Yet the arrogance of modern-day people has created a "god" in the image and likeness of them. We are so self-deceived and deceived by the enemy that we actually think we have the authority to redefine truth. We can no more define truth than we can command the earth to stand still in its orbit around the sun. We can't define truth because God alone is the standard of truth—but it *is* essential we discover the truth.

Here's the point: It is up to us to adjust our watch to match the standard, not to try to get the standard to match our watch.

We have to adjust our lives to God's standard instead of trying to distort God's standard to match our lives. There is one place you can go for the absolute standard of truth and reality. That's why God has given us the Bible. It's the gold standard measuring rod of reality for what is true. Truth is not determined by your vote, my vote, the majority vote, or public opinion. It is not the opinions of your friends or a TV talk show host or a celebrity or whoever else you are listening to. God alone is the majority, and He defines truth. His truth is irreversible and completely unshakable. You may hate the truth, you may make fun of the truth, you may choose not to believe the truth and choose to ignore it, but in the end, truth is still the truth.

You need to *tune in to God to get the truth and His standard of reality.* I'm not going to try to change God's standard to match my life as so many people try to do. I'm going to change my life to match God's standard. That's what it means to put on the belt of truth and to stand.

You are ready to go to battle because now you have a firm foundation from which to wage war—you have absolute truth. Satan doesn't want you to know the truth because knowledge is power. Therefore, he will attack and distort the truth and try to get you to deny the truth. He'll do anything he can to conceal the truth because he does not want you to have it.

Christ brings you liberty, power, and victory!

Satan doesn't want you to be free—he wants you to stay in captivity. He's a liar by nature, and his lies hold you in captivity and slavery. It's Christ who brings you liberty, power, and victory. Jesus says in John 8:32, *"You shall know the truth, and the truth shall make you free."*

CHAPTER 7

WHAT YOU DON'T KNOW CAN KILL YOU

My people are destroyed for lack of knowledge... (Hosea 4:6).

Nearly 3,000 years ago, the prophet Hosea lamented the same problem we see all around us today—God's people are being taken out by spiritual snipers because they lack the knowledge that comes from studying God's Word and getting it firmly rooted in their spirits. We're living in the time of Hosea 4:6. There's the problem. The average Christian is destroyed for lack of knowledge.

Remember, Satan is a thief who comes to steal, kill, and destroy. He destroys the people of God when they lack knowledge of the Word of God. In this day and age, so many Christians have a superficial, shallow understanding of the written Word; therefore, they have a superficial, shallow relationship with the Living Word. That is why I believe this generation of Christians is the most anemic, powerless, defeated generation of Christians who has ever lived.

Here's the point: You cannot have a deep, abiding relationship with the Living Word if you don't have a deep, abiding knowledge of the written Word.

Tragically, we're living in a time when this generation of Christians is all but biblically illiterate. Paul described our current age in his letter to his spiritual son, Timothy:

> *For the time will come when they will not endure sound doctrine, but according to their own desires, because they have itching ears, they will heap up for themselves teachers; and they will turn their ears away from the truth, and be turned aside to fables* (2 Timothy 4:3-4).

So many pastors all across the United States have bought into this consumer-driven Christianity and the itching ears of the people; consequently, they preach nothing but pabulum. Most preaching in America is nothing more than motivational speaking with a few Bible verses sprinkled in along the way. God says down through the ages, *"My people are destroyed for lack of knowledge"* because the average Christian isn't learning the Word of God! If you don't know the Word of God, you are easy prey for the enemy.

Knowledge is power. Fortunately, there are still many good churches in the United States getting it done and preaching the Word of God. Knowing the Bible is crucial to living victoriously. The Bible gives you the knowledge you need to win against the enemy. Satan's lies are subtle; all it takes is a little, itty-bitty lie, sprinkled with the truth, to destroy you. *"My people are destroyed for lack of knowledge."*

Many Christians in the U.S. form their belief system by taking some solid Christian teaching, mixing it with a little New Age theology, a little secular psychology, and a little worldly philosophy. They take some solid biblical teaching and mix that in with some false teaching from what falls under the banner of orthodoxy. This salad bar mentality of deciding what is true and what is not, depending on what is palatable to you, leads to nothing more than a platter full of poison. It is truth seasoned with lies.

DISCERNING TRUTH FROM ERROR

Not only *can* you know the truth, it is essential that you *know* the truth. How do you discern truth from error? The very first thing you must put on in the morning is the belt of truth by spending time renewing your mind in the Word. Having belted your waist with truth means that you must become so familiar with the truth that you instantly recognize a lie no matter how small or imperceptible or subtle.

I used to stand guard as a SWAT cop with the Secret Service when politicians and dignitaries came into town. They would sometimes pair us up with a Secret Service agent on security detail, and we would stand in one place sometimes all day. It gave us lots of time for conversation. The Secret Service does more than guard high-ranking politicians and dignitaries. A lot of what they do is investigate counterfeiting. I had always heard Secret Service agents learn to spot a counterfeit bill by handling real money.

As I was passing the time one day on a security detail, I asked a Secret Service agent if that was true. He said they spent hour after hour handling real U.S. currency. They became so familiar with every detail of the real thing that they could quickly spot a counterfeit.

Satan is a master counterfeiter. He counterfeits all that God is and all that God does. In the same way a Secret Service agent becomes so familiar with U.S. currency from many hours of handling the real thing and can quickly spot a counterfeit (even blindfolded!), so you and I must become familiar with the truth.

You must spend time in the Word of God learning it so you can instantly recognize any counterfeit Satan brings to defeat and enslave you. It is not enough just to know the Word of God, you have to *believe* the Word of God and allow it to form your entire belief system. It's not trying to get the Word of God to fit within your belief system; you have to allow the Word of God to *form* your belief system. That means if I think one thing and God's Word says another, I'm wrong and God is right. We have a final authority that is the standard of reality, and it should shape our entire belief system because we are going to battle.

Strengthen your mind by immersing your mind in God's infallible Word.

The apostle Peter makes a statement similar to what Paul says in First Peter 1:13, *"Gird up the loins of your mind."* In exactly the same way a Roman soldier would roll up his skirt and tuck it and tie it into that belt, girding up his loins as they were preparing for battle, Peter says you need to get ready for battle by renewing and strengthening your mind. Remember, the battle is in the mind. You strengthen your mind with God's truth by immersing your mind in God's infallible Word.

The Roman belt was also similar to a girdle. A girdle is not very flattering; it is meant to firm up the unfit parts of our mid-section. Peter is saying to gird up the loins of our mind, those areas of our thought life that are weak and out of shape.

Here's the point: If you have a soft mind and a flabby faith, it's time to gird it up before you go to battle.

If you have ever seen powerlifters on TV, you know they are huge and powerful and strong, and they are lifting enormous amounts of weight. Most of them have a big belly. They cinch up their bellies with their weight belt. They're girding up their loins. In other words, that belt isn't just meant for hanging stuff on it—it was also meant for keeping stuff in. In the same way, the Roman soldier had a belt that wasn't just for hanging stuff on it. It was made to keep other stuff from hanging out. It was firming up the soft and vulnerable spots of his body.

You gird up the loins of your mind as a Roman soldier would gird up his hips. In today's vernacular, you might say, "Roll up your sleeves." If I told you to roll up your sleeves, you would immediately understand that it's time to get to work. We're going to get it, we're going to hit it, we're going to get strengthened, and we're going to get toughened.

Before the U.S. military sends any soldiers into combat, they go through basic training where they will be worked hard. Why? Because they have to toughen up the soldiers. They are going to run off the fat and flab. Soldiers are going to be part of a lean, mean fighting machine after completing basic training.

ARMED AND DANGEROUS

Paul was saying the same thing Peter was saying. Before you engage in warfare, I want you to be armed and dangerous. You have everything you need to win against all the power of the enemy. You can be a lean, mean fighting machine, but you have to get rid of some of the mental fat. You have to get rid of some of the spiritual flab, and this is how you do it: *"Do not be conformed to this world, but be transformed by the renewing of your mind..."* (Romans 12:2). Whatever controls that thing between your ears will control you.

Peter and Paul are saying that some of us still have a fat mind that is full of flabby thoughts and a flabby faith. We are not ready to stand in warfare and engage in combat with an enemy as powerful as Satan. We fill our minds with the fat and the flab of this world by watching soap operas, the "rom coms," and sitcoms full of sexual innuendos and immorality, worldly philosophy and Satanic ideology. And then we wonder why we can't win the war within. Peter says to *"gird up the loins of your mind."* It's time to get rid of our soft, sinful way of thinking by renewing our minds daily.

The moment you were saved, your Spirit was reborn, but your mind is never reborn. That's why over and over again the Bible says your mind must be renewed. For that to happen, you have to begin replacing your thoughts with God's thoughts. This is critical because Satan will use how you respond to circumstances, temptations, trials, and tribulations to control you and keep you in slavery. If you have not girded your mind, Satan will defeat you through unforgiveness, bitterness, guilt, fear, worry, or lust.

We have programmed our minds through years and years of life in this wicked world to respond in certain ways, at certain times, and with certain people through the trials, tribulations, and temptations we face. We often allow those old thought patterns to control us rather than allowing God to be in control.

If you want to live in Christ's liberty, you have to allow God to deprogram your mind by taking out all the ungodly data and putting in new data. You do that by immersing your mind in God's thoughts until they become your thoughts. You say, "God, will You take the Word of God in the hands of the Spirit of God to make me more like the Son of God?" That's how you begin to see your life transformed. It begins inwardly before He transforms you outwardly. You learn to think more like God.

Philippians 2:5 says, *"Let this mind be in you which was also in Christ Jesus."* Let God's thoughts become your thoughts, and I can promise you will win the battle that rages within. That's how you buckle the belt of truth and prepare for battle.

PART IV

WAGING WAR AGAINST THE ENEMY

THE BREASTPLATE OF RIGHTEOUSNESS

Finally, my brethren, be strong in the Lord and in the power of His might. Put on the whole armor of God, that you may be able to stand against the wiles of the devil. For we do not wrestle against flesh and blood, but against principalities, against powers, against the rulers of the darkness of this age, against spiritual hosts of wickedness in the heavenly places. Therefore take up the whole armor of God, that you may be able to withstand in the evil day, and having done all, to stand. Stand therefore, having girded your waist with truth, having put on the breastplate of righteousness, and having shod your feet with the preparation of the gospel of peace; above all, taking the shield of faith with which you will be able to quench all the fiery darts of the wicked one. And take the helmet of salvation, and the sword of the Spirit, which is the word of God (Ephesians 6:10-17).

I was shocked when I heard the news. I had only been off the rookie "break-in" period a short time as a member of the KCPD when one of the officers I was friends with was involved in a shooting. It's what we trained for, spending six months in the police academy before ever hitting the streets. It's something we all knew was a possibility when we chose law enforcement as a career. Fortunately, having to fire our weapon at someone is fairly rare. In fact, some officers never have to take aim and shoot their entire careers. The movies and cop sitcoms make it look like it's all in a day's work, but that is hardly the case in reality.

When a shooting occurs, it's always extremely sobering. It's about life and death. This time it was especially sobering because my officer friend was hit in the chest. Fortunately, he was wearing his Kevlar bulletproof vest and it probably saved his life.

The second piece of armor Paul tells us to put on after the belt of truth is the breastplate of righteousness. It's not hard to figure out why the Roman soldier had a breastplate. Ancient warriors used a breastplate for the same reason modern soldiers and police officers wear bulletproof vests. Since its invention in the 1970s, the Kevlar vest has saved the lives of thousands of men and women in law enforcement and the military.

Because vital life-sustaining organs are in our chest, the breastplate is one of the most important pieces of a Roman soldier's armor. You can't wait until you're in the heat of battle to decide to put on your armor. It's too late then. You will never see a police officer in the throes of a gun battle saying, "Wait a minute, time out, I have to put on my bulletproof vest! Hang on, stop shooting…that's not fair!" You have to suit up before you face your adversary, or you will lose every time.

"Put on the whole armor of God." For Paul to write it twice in the course of three verses must mean it's important, and he doesn't want the reader to miss it. In Ephesians 6:11, Paul writes, *"Put on the*

whole armor of God, that you may be able to stand against the wiles of the devil." He writes it again in verse 13, *"Take up the whole armor of God."* He's reminding you that it doesn't do any good to go charging into battle if you are wearing only one or two pieces of the armor. You need to dress for battle, complete with the whole armor. Don't leave any of the pieces at home. Every piece of Christ's armor works together to bring about your success in battle. Each piece is essential to your very survival.

> Christ's armor works together for your success in battle.

You probably wouldn't dream of leaving the house in the morning and going into a public place half-dressed, but spiritually, we do it almost every day. We go into the battles of life and of this world half-dressed and unprepared for battle. Before you even get out of bed and your feet hit the floor in the morning, you had better put on the armor, because a lot of mornings the battle has begun the moment you open your eyes.

The only reason anybody would leave without being fully dressed for battle is because they don't take the battle seriously. Far too many Christians don't take the opposition seriously. We read what Paul wrote, but we don't take it literally. Paul is not writing about some fictional conflict like we see in a movie. He is writing about a literal battle. Paul makes it clear that we do not wrestle against flesh and blood. We are at war with fallen angels, principalities, and

WEAPONS OF OUR WARFARE

powers. It can be a catastrophic mistake in warfare not to take your opposition seriously.

The purpose of the breastplate is obvious. A Roman soldier would wear his breastplate because it protected the vital, life-sustaining organs—specifically his lungs and especially his heart. Ancient archers would aim for the enemy's heart because they knew it was an instant kill shot. Roman soldiers would go into battle wearing their breastplate, either made of metal or thick leather, apart from which they could not survive or have success in battle.

God has given us a breastplate for the very same reason. His breastplate is essential to your survival, and it is essential to your success in battle against the wickedness of this fallen world.

> Our breastplate is unique from all others—
> it is a breastplate of righteousness.

What is it about righteousness that has anything to do with a breastplate? The Bible teaches we have no righteousness of our own; as human beings, we are not righteous. Romans 3:10 says, *"There is none righteous, no, not one."* To be righteous means to be right in the eyes of God. It means to be holy. It means to be without sin. It means to be pure.

GOD'S STANDARD

God's standard is sinless perfection. You may think you are righteous compared to somebody else, but you are not righteous compared to

God. The Bible teaches that you are not righteous because you are right in somebody else's eyes or you are right in your own eyes. You are righteous only by being right in God's eyes. And to be right in God's eyes means that you have never, ever sinned.

> *Therefore, just as through one man* [Adam] *sin entered the world, and death through sin, and thus death spread to all men, because all sinned* (Romans 5:12).

Romans 3:23 says that *"all have sinned and fall short of the glory of God."* Because we have all been born as members of Adam's fallen race, we have Adam's fallen nature. That means we are sinners by nature and sinners by choice. You probably know of somebody with a self-righteous attitude. They somehow think they are better than everybody else. They have a holier-than-thou attitude like the Pharisees in Jesus' day. They don't smoke, don't cuss, don't chew, and don't run with girls who do. They think, *You know, I'm actually a pretty good person. I'm definitely better than most.*

> *If we say that we have no sin, we deceive ourselves, and the truth is not in us* (1 John 1:8).

It doesn't matter who you are or what you have done; there is not one person on earth who is righteous. Heaven is a place of sinless, righteous perfection, and nothing less can ever enter in. As flawed, fallen human beings, we all possess a flawed nature. That is why God sent heaven's righteous One, His eternal, sinless Son, who never, ever sinned.

Second Corinthians 5:21 tells us that, *"He made Him* [Jesus] *who knew no sin to be sin for us, that we might become the righteousness of God in Him."* God put all of His sinlessness on us and put all of our sinfulness on Him. On the cross of Calvary, He literally traded places with us. A legal transaction took place so that we can become the righteousness of God in Christ—not because we're righteous, we're not righteous in ourselves, but now we can be righteous in Him.

Here's the point: You may be a pretty good person, but you are not righteous. You may be a moral person, but you are not righteous. You may be a religious person, but you are not righteous. You may be a nice person, but you are not righteous. To be righteous means you are sinless.

Sin is breaking God's law, and whenever you break a law, there is a legal penalty that must be paid. God says in Romans 6:23, *"The wages of sin is death."* God brought down the gavel and found Adam guilty. Adam's penalty was death—ours was too.

Christ had to die to pay the penalty for our sin. No one else could do it for us. There was a punishment that would ensue, and the sinless One traded places with the sinful ones on the cross of Calvary. The innocent died for the guilty. God placed our sin upon Him; He placed our blame upon Him. He took our penalty and our punishment, and He in turn placed His righteousness on us. He died in our place so that we can become the righteousness of God in Him.

With the penalty of our sin now legally paid, God declares us righteous. He declares us sinless. He looks at us as though we have never sinned. In the criminal justice system, it's called having your record expunged. That means somebody who breaks the law legally owes the penalty of the law. But if that person can meet certain conditions, the judge and the court can decide to have their record expunged. It will be erased as if it never happened.

We broke the law. We legally were under the penalty of the law, but because the conditions were met of the law and Jesus died in our place and paid the punishment for us, He has expunged our record. In the eyes of God, if you are a child of God, it's as though you've never sinned. Perhaps for some that may not be that big of a deal, but for us big-time sinners, that's a really big deal!

In God's eyes, if you are a child of God, it's as though you've never sinned.

Legally, the penalty of our sin has been paid in the eyes of God, so He declares us righteous and sinless. Romans 8:30 calls it being *"justified."* The moment you were born again by faith in Jesus Christ, God took the breastplate of righteousness and placed it on your life. Isaiah 59:17 says Jesus Christ *"put on righteousness as a breastplate."* He took His breastplate of righteousness, placed it on us, took all of our sin, and placed it on Him. Now we can be called the righteousness of God in Him. That means positionally in Christ, you are as righteous as the Son of God! Did you get that? Underline it! As a child of God, you are as righteous in the eyes of God as the sinless Son of God!

The amazing thing in the plan of God is that *the* Son of God became like sons of men so that sons and daughters of men could become the children of God. Wow! The goal now that you are a child of God is to become like THE Son of God, *"to be conformed to the image of His Son"* (Romans 8:29) and to be *"holy and without blame"* (Ephesians 1:4).

This is where the breastplate of righteousness comes in. You can be experientially everything you already are positionally. Salvation isn't just a one-and-done proposition but rather a process. You are forever saved from sin's penalty. *"For whoever calls on the name of the Lord shall be saved"* (Romans 10:13). Now God wants to save you from sin's power. In the eyes of God, it's just as if I never sinned. That is justification.

SANCTIFICATION

Now you need to be delivered from the power of sin through sanctification. Sanctification is simply a theological term that means to be set apart. When you are first saved, you experience positional sanctification. God has set you apart from sin's power. The goal is to become practically who you already are positionally, which is holy and without blame, sinless like the Son of God.

It is a process, and practically speaking, you'll never be sinless in this world—that is what the Bible calls glorification (Romans 8:30). Someday you are going to die, you are going to go to heaven, and then you will become literally, in every capacity, exactly like Him.

Just as a breastplate protected the Roman soldier's heart, the breastplate of righteousness protects your heart. Whenever you see the word "heart" in the Bible, it rarely has to do with that little muscle pumping blood throughout your body. Rather, the word "heart" is referring to the soul. The heart and soul are the control center of who you are. The soul represents the mind, the will, and the emotions—your thoughts, your meditations, your decisions, your direction. Always remember, you are *a* child of God so that you can become more and more like *the* Son of God. That's the goal of the Christian life.

CHAPTER 8

A HOLY HEART IS A HEALTHY HEART

Keep [guard] *your heart with all diligence, for out of it spring the issues of life* (Proverbs 4:23).

The Bible tells us we are prone to sin because there's a problem with human beings, a problem of the human heart. Jeremiah 17:9 says, *"The heart is deceitful above all things, and desperately wicked; who can know it?"* We can't even know our own heart because it deceives even us.

We're desperately wicked by nature, but when you trusted Jesus Christ as your Lord and Savior, you were born again (John 3:3). God's Spirit literally came to live inside of you. His Spirit gives life to your spirit; your spirit is now one with His Spirit. Your heart was once sinful, but He gives you a new heart—the very heart of God. You now have God's nature.

Ezekiel 36:26 says, *"I will give you a new heart and put a new spirit within you...."* As a born-again, blood-bought child of God, you have been given a new heart and a new nature that is holy and righteous, and it loves what is pure and good, positionally.

The goal is for that to become your practical reality. The reason that is so difficult is because as long as you are still stuck in this flesh, you still have that old heart. You still have that old nature that every single day so easily grows cold and selfish, is quick to sin, and easily succumbs to temptation. That is why over and over again Scripture tells us to guard our hearts.

Now you can understand why it's so important to put on the breastplate of righteousness daily to guard your heart. It is why Proverbs 4:23 tells us to *"Keep* [guard] *your heart with all diligence, for out of it spring the issues of life."* Living with purity and integrity is how you keep on your breastplate of righteousness, and it is how you guard your heart daily.

It's learning to guard your heart by guarding the eye gate. Job 31:1 tells us, *"I have made a covenant with my eyes...."* Job made a covenant with his eyes not to look at any unclean or sinful thing. He was guarding his heart by guarding his eyes. Millions of people worldwide, both men and women, are enslaved to pornography. Their hearts are now poisoned wells of depravity and sensuality. What goes in through the eyes eventually poisons the entire well.

Not only that, but we need to make a covenant with our ears. The ears are another gateway to our heart. It's the music we listen to and the gossip that defiles us. Everything we see, hear, and experience in life has a way of affecting our heart for either good or evil.

Here's the point: The breastplate of righteousness is to guard your heart from sin because the life you live outwardly is the summation of your heart condition inwardly.

Satan knows that life flows out of our hearts. That is why it is so important to put on the breastplate of righteousness to keep our hearts pure from the pollution of this world and the seeds of sin the enemy sows.

A life that is healthy and happy is a reflection of a heart that is healthy and holy. A healthy, holy heart brings forth a happy, healthy life. A life shredded by sin outwardly is a reflection of a heart that has been soiled by sin inwardly. You live your life above the surface in a way that reflects the condition of your heart below the surface. That's why you have a breastplate to put on every single day to guard your heart from anything that is unrighteous.

Satan wants to soil, pollute, corrupt, and destroy your heart because out of the heart spring the issues of life. Your heart encompasses your entire belief system—your attitude, your emotions, your thought patterns, your vision, your values, your decisions—and the direction you take inwardly. Satan wants to take a shot at your heart because he knows you will become outwardly whoever you are inwardly.

Some Bibles translate *"issues of life"* in Proverbs 4:23 as the *"wellspring* [source] *of life."* When I was a young boy, I went to my grandma and grandpa's farm in southern Missouri. Today we would say it was "off the grid." I was ten years of age before they had running water. You may think that's rough living, but not for a ten-year-old boy. I thought I was in heaven! No bath for three days. It just didn't get much better than that.

I would stay for a week or more at a time in the summer. Every day I would go with my grandpa to a little spring down in the "holler" behind the house. We would take milk cans with us to draw water from a spring of clear, cold, pristine water. We would bend down and drink from the stream. To this day it might be the best water I've ever tasted. The reason it was so clean, clear, and pristine on the surface is because the wellspring underneath the surface was just as clean, clear, and pristine.

King Solomon, the author of the book of Proverbs, probably was thinking about just such a spring when he wrote in Proverbs 4:23 (NIV), *"Above all else, guard your heart, for everything you do flows from it."*

Whatever you are outwardly is a reflection of the river of water that dwells inwardly.

Your life right now is either pure, clean, and pristine, and you are living what Jesus calls "life abundantly," or your life right now is muddy, murky, and dingy. Who you are and the things you do in your day-to-day life are reflections of what you are inside. God, in His infinite love, has given us the breastplate of righteousness to guard that wellspring of life.

Behaviors are always a reflection of belief. You will do what you believe. Right beliefs lead to righteous behavior; right attitudes lead to righteous actions. Righteousness begins with the wellspring of your life. Just as a spring of water bubbling up above the surface is clear and clean, it is clear and clean at the wellspring. It all begins below the surface where nobody else can see.

This is why Satan wants to attack your heart every single day. The apostle Paul referred to those attacks as the *"fiery darts of the wicked one."* Ancient archers aimed for the heart because it was a guaranteed kill shot. Do you understand that Satan and his demonic archers are aiming for your heart? If your life has no abundance or vibrancy, it's because of the condition of its source of life—your heart.

Here's the point: Every day Satan wants to put a poison dart through your heart because he knows your heart is the source of life.

Sin is poison to your heart and soul. Satan wants to introduce something unrighteous to your heart. He wants to corrupt your heart and fill it with bitterness, unforgiveness, or anger. He wants to fill your heart with lies or lust or pornography or immorality. He wants to fill your heart with unrighteousness so that you cannot live righteously.

He's aiming at your heart to poison, contaminate, and control it because whoever or whatever controls your heart controls you. Every day he's taking shots at your heart. Sadly, in this day and age, he has a lot of help. He's taking a shot at your heart when you're surfing the Internet late at night. He's there when you're flipping channels and linger too long on something you run across that you know you have no business watching.

Women and men are equally vulnerable when attempting to go about their day without guarding their hearts. For you, it may be the temptation to join in with your gossiping neighbor or linger too long at the water cooler with that oh-so-friendly coworker. You're just as vulnerable to the smorgasbord of filth on TV, the Internet, and social media.

Read this carefully: *you take off your breastplate by choosing to do wrong when you know what is right.* When you choose to do wrong when you know what God says is right, you expose your heart to the enemy. You are taking off your breastplate and exposing your heart.

The devil wants to put a poison dart through your heart!

I've known for a long time to guard my heart by being careful about what movies or television shows I watch. So many of them are filled with sexual innuendos, promiscuity, and immorality. My TV viewing is usually either sports or news. Unfortunately, we can't always even watch the commercials. Occasionally, I'll watch an outdoors show or something on the History channel.

A while back, I started watching one particular sitcom. It was a real cultural phenomenon. I'd heard about it for several years. On top of that I kept hearing people I considered to be very godly, mature believers—even other pastors—talking about how much they loved this show. I would hear them bragging about binge-watching the reruns. I decided to give it a chance. I thought, *Maybe I'm just a prude and need to loosen up.*

So I started watching this popular TV sitcom. After an episode or two, I finally got it. It was hilarious! I found myself repeatedly laughing out loud! I even started to binge-watch previous seasons in my leisure time. The characters were hilarious. The scriptwriters were genius. There was, of course, the occasional and sometimes more than occasional sexual joke, innuendo, or sexually suggestive scene. I would squirm a little and then shrug it off. For the most part it was clean.

But then during one episode, I found myself laughing out loud at something God hates! It was another sexual, suggestive innuendo.

Honestly, it was really funny, but it had to do with something that makes God angry. It was depravity. In Scripture, God makes it clear that He considers this specific thing an abomination. Then it hit me—or more specifically, the Holy Spirit hit me. I thought to myself, *What am I doing? Here I am laughing at something I know God hates!* I quietly sat there on my couch as I realized: *At one time, I never would have done this.*

Right then and there, I said, "Lord, forgive me that I have treated so flippantly things You consider depravity." I turned off the show and haven't watched it since. I realized that day that I had taken off my breastplate of righteousness. I had exposed my heart, and Satan shot it with a poison dart. The show had subtly poisoned the wellspring of my heart.

We can't live godly lives when we fill our hearts full of ungodliness.

Sin gives the devil the advantage on a silver platter. When you take a step off the high ground by even one small compromise with sin, you are giving Satan a toehold in your heart. Keep going and that toehold becomes a foothold. Pretty soon that foothold will become a handhold, and the handhold eventually becomes a stronghold (2 Corinthians 10:4). A stronghold is an area of your life that Satan now completely controls. It is ground that was once won and ruled by Jesus that has been won back and is now ruled by Satan.

Remember, the goal of warfare is to take enemy-held territory. When you give up pieces of your heart, you are giving back ground to the enemy that Jesus won at Calvary. Protect the high ground of your heart at all cost.

PROTECT YOUR HEART

You already have righteousness positionally that Satan cannot take from you. There is nothing he can do that will undo what Christ has already done. What he can do and wants to do is rob you of your practical righteousness through the decisions you make and the things you do. When you choose to do wrong when you know what is right, you gradually take off your breastplate and expose your heart to the enemy.

This is why so many in the Church today are controlled by sin and Satan. They didn't get there in a day. It was by making one decision at a time and taking off their breastplate over and over and over again. The devil can't take it by force, but it can be surrendered by the one who wears it.

The Great Wall of China is still known as one of the Seven Ancient Wonders of the World. At 4,500 miles in length, it is so enormous it can be seen from outer space. It was built by the ancient Chinese to protect them from outside invaders. In the first one hundred years of the wall's existence, the enemies of China never once conquered the wall. They never went over it or through it; but three times China's enemies went in because three times the gate was unlocked from within by a gatekeeper who accepted a bribe.

In exactly the same manner, Satan wants to get in, but he cannot penetrate the fortress God has given you; he cannot penetrate the armor. You have a breastplate of righteousness—the righteousness of the Lord Jesus Christ. For the enemy to gain entry to your heart, it must be opened from within. That's exactly what we do every time we choose to sin. When we know what is right and we choose to do wrong, we open our heart and expose it to the enemy. And he desires nothing more than to put a dart through our heart.

Here's the point: You are the gatekeeper to your heart, and you are the only one with the key.

You keep your breastplate on simply by choosing to walk in the righteousness of the Lord Jesus Christ. You receive this breastplate by faith in Jesus Christ, and you wear it by obedience to Jesus Christ. It's a choice with every single decision to walk in obedience, to make decisions that reflect your position, and to keep your breastplate on or take it off.

You have this righteousness already, positionally. You wear your breastplate of righteousness by choosing to do right even when you are tempted to do what is wrong. It's with your heart that you'll either choose divorce or you will choose to be married until death do you part. It's with your heart that you will choose faithfulness or infidelity in your marriage. It's with your heart that you will either choose purity or sexual promiscuity.

Your decisions are reflections of the inner condition of the heart.

Your decisions are reflections of the inner condition of the heart. Your decisions make your positional righteousness your practical, daily reality so that you can live what Jesus calls abundant life. Let your condition reflect your position through your decisions. Your decisions set your direction, and your direction sets your destination. Where do you want to be in life? What kind of life do you want to live? You are going somewhere because life is a journey.

Your destiny—where you will be ten years from now, the person you will be twenty years from now—is simply a summation of the decisions you make today. Guard your heart with all diligence, with determination and tenacity. Decisions set your direction, your direction sets your destination, and it all begins with the wellspring of your heart.

CHAPTER 9

THE WILES OF
THE DEVIL

For we do not wrestle against flesh and blood, but against principalities, against powers, against the rulers of the darkness of this age, against spiritual hosts of wickedness in the heavenly places (Ephesians 6:12).

The screeching sound of shredded metal could have awakened the dead. Little did they know that very soon the living would be dead. It was April 14, 1912, and it was the maiden voyage of the much-celebrated Titanic. She was touted as the unsinkable ship—indestructible and completely invincible. Now the unthinkable was happening. How could something so secure and so stable be in such a desperate situation?

The source, you see, was the danger beneath the surface—a place nobody could see—the hidden recesses invisible to common sight and the powers of observation. Equally to blame was the egotistical, overconfidence of the crew.

So it was on the black, frigid waters that night on the North Atlantic that the Titanic sank—the casualty of an iceberg hidden beneath the surface. Researchers would later discover the iceberg that caused six gashes in the hull and destroyed the ship was not a threat that could be seen. The part of the iceberg that could be seen above the surface was not the real threat. The Titanic was sunk by ice below the surface they never saw coming.

The most dangerous enemy is the one you cannot see!

What is true of the Titanic is true of our own lives. Our real enemy is not the enemy we can see, but the enemy we cannot see.

The fallen angels, or principalities and powers as Paul calls them, are the rulers of the darkness of this world. Satan hides in the shadows just below the surface. Jesus said he's a thief. A thief doesn't call to tell us when he's coming. He wants to sink us into a sea of sin and drown and destroy us in a sea of sorrow—just like those on the Titanic who thought they were unsinkable.

It's usually when we're not watching and when we're not ready that we get hit with something we never saw coming. That's why First

Peter 5:8 says, *"Be sober, be vigilant...."* Always stay on guard; never let your guard down.

Here's the point: You will never reach a place of spiritual maturity where you are beyond Satan's reach.

You never reach some pinnacle of spiritual victory where you can never go back into captivity. You can never say, "I'm completely free and Satan has no way of touching me." Be on guard...be sober, be vigilant.

When we think we're the strongest, we're actually the most vulnerable. That's when we let our guard down. Our strongest and most fortified moments against the enemy are sometimes when we feel the weakest. Awareness of our weakness is what drives us to Jesus. Yes, Satan is like a lion that preys on the weak, but he also preys on the strong. Sometimes when you are feeling the most invincible, like those on the Titanic, you get hit by something you never saw coming. You think you are strong, so you let down your guard.

Awareness of our weakness is what drives us to Jesus.

My training in the Kansas City Police Academy taught me something I've never forgotten. We were taught that statistically when an officer is killed in the line of duty by an armed assailant or adversary, he has an average of seven years on the street. He's a very seasoned and very tenured officer.

What amazed me at the time was that I logically thought it would be the rookie, the one who is new on the street and doesn't have the experience who would be most vulnerable to an armed attack. But it made sense the more I thought about it. When you're a rookie and come out of the Academy, you are on guard. You think everybody has a gun and everybody's going to shoot at you. You don't want to get pulled over by the rookie. If a little old lady blows a stop sign, he would be the one shouting with gun drawn, "Get your hands up, get your hands up!" The poor little old lady is saying, "I'm sorry officer, please don't shoot." It's not the rookie that's going to get shot because he's on guard.

Seven years later, he has pulled over hundreds and hundreds and hundreds of cars, and nothing has ever happened. Then he pulls over that one and gets hit by something he never saw coming. What happened? He let his guard down. Spiritually, it's exactly the same. We can never be unaware—not one day, one moment, one second.

When you look in the Bible, you can see all the heroes of the faith. A lot of them started well, but if you read the end of the story of their lives, they didn't all end well. We should never say we're beyond the reach of Satan. We need to stay vigilant at all times. We're learning how to stay on guard and how to dress for battle because every day we need to realize that we are in warfare with a real and very powerful enemy. He's coming after us, and he wants to destroy us and take us out of the battle. We have to remain watchful because Satan will hit us when we're not ready and not watching.

Let me remind you, as a child of God, you are armed by God and a danger to the enemy. You are a threat to the enemy, and he is opposing you because you are a threat to his kingdom. This is a battle of opposing kings and opposing kingdoms. It's Light versus darkness, and he wants to take you out and stop you because you are a threat to him. The good news is we don't have to live in defeat; we can live dynamically. We don't have to be vanquished; we can live victoriously.

Jesus said you can live life abundantly because God has already given you everything you need to live in victory over all the power of the adversary. When I was on the police force, we were given all the equipment we needed to be prepared for any situation. We were equipped for whatever we encountered. We had all kinds of things hanging from our hips so we would have everything we needed. God has given you everything you need as well. He has equipped you in exactly the same way, with armor and weapons.

THE WHOLE ARMOR

My friend, General Jerry Boykin, graciously endorsed this book. General Boykin knows a thing or two about combat—both physical combat and spiritual combat. He is a true man of God besides being one of the most decorated warriors in recent U.S. military history. He was one of the original members of Delta Force formed in 1978, which remains to this day as arguably the most elite unit of Special Operations warriors in the U.S. military. He rose through the ranks to Lieutenant General and commanded all U.S. Special Forces before finishing his stellar military career in the Pentagon. For thirty-six years he was living the news while the rest of the world only heard about it the next day or saw it portrayed in movies.

The battle of Mogadishu on October 3, 1993, has been well documented in both the book and the movie, *Black Hawk Down*. General Boykin was there. Over dinner one night, I asked him what he thought of the movie and how realistic it was. He said it was largely a very accurate portrayal of that horrible day in 1993. Some of America's most elite soldiers—Army Rangers and other Special Forces—were shot to shreds by guerilla fighters of a very evil Somali warlord. Nineteen U.S.

soldiers died and seventy-three were wounded during an eighteen-hour battle they anticipated lasting only a few minutes.

These elite warriors were well-armed and they were well-trained, but some of them made a critical mistake. To lighten their load, they took the heavy plastic plate out of their Kevlar vest that was meant to stop a high-powered round fired from an AK-47. Worst of all, they left behind their night vision goggles. They anticipated their mission lasting only a few minutes. They never dreamed they would be there all day and all night. Once darkness fell over the city, they lost all advantage over the enemy.

General Boykin said what the movie doesn't show is they had made six missions into the city prior to that fateful seventh mission. They had encountered very little resistance, and the only casualties they had endured up to that point were two soldiers with such superficial wounds they were literally treated with Band-Aids.

These elite warriors anticipated this seventh mission going like the first six, but this time they walked into an ambush. The enemy was ready. Within minutes, one hundred U.S. warriors found themselves surrounded by ten thousand Somalis with AK47s and rocket-propelled grenades. These were some of the most courageous, bravest men in the military, and they deserve our honor—but leaving behind critical pieces of equipment cost them dearly.

Now you understand why Paul tells us twice in the space of three verses to put on the *"whole armor of God"*—not just the parts you feel like wearing. The enemy is trying to ambush you every day. It's what Paul calls the wiles, or schemes, of the devil. Every single day the enemy is watching and waiting for an opportunity to ambush you. He is setting up an ambush for you at this very moment.

That's what Paul is driving home in verse 11 when he tells us, *"Put on the whole armor of God, that you may be able to stand against the wiles of the devil"*—the schemes, the snares, the ambushes, the traps of the devil. Unless you have put on the whole armor of God, you will not be ready when you find yourself in the heat of battle. It will be too late to call "timeout" so you can go back and get in your prayer closet with your Bible and put on the critical equipment you left behind.

Many of those who served in Vietnam were often the point person on jungle patrols. They learned to sense when the enemy was near— not because of what they could see, but because of what they couldn't see. They learned to listen to the jungle. Suddenly, the jungle would become completely quiet. The birds wouldn't be singing or flying, and they knew the enemy was near and an ambush was imminent.

Learn not only to see life through your physical eyes, but through your spiritual eyes as well.

God has given you that very same ability. You have the Spirit of God living within you. Yes, we *"walk in the flesh"* according to Second Corinthians 10:3, but *"we do not war according to the flesh."* You have to learn not only to see life through your physical eyes, but through your spiritual eyes as well. God has given you spiritual eyes to see what cannot be physically seen. He wants you to know your enemy and understand when you are in the middle of an ambush so you will be ready.

Make this your heart's cry every day:

I will let nothing unrighteous enter my life to corrupt my righteous position in Christ. I will wear Your breastplate of righteousness daily, Lord. I will choose righteous decisions to reflect my righteous position so that Your spiritual identity will become a daily reality in my life. I will not expose my heart to the enemy, and I will choose to walk in virtue, honesty, and integrity.

PART V

KEEPING THE PEACE
IN A WORLD WAR

THE GOSPEL OF PEACE

Finally, my brethren, be strong in the Lord and in the power of His might. Put on the whole armor of God, that you may be able to stand against the wiles of the devil. For we do not wrestle against flesh and blood, but against principalities, against powers, against the rulers of the darkness of this age, against spiritual hosts of wickedness in the heavenly places. Therefore take up the whole armor of God, that you may be able to withstand in the evil day, and having done all, to stand. Stand therefore, having girded your waist with truth, having put on the breastplate of righteousness, and having shod your feet with the preparation of the gospel of peace; above all, taking the shield of faith with which you will be able to quench all the fiery darts of the wicked one. And take the helmet of salvation, and the sword of the Spirit, which is the word of God (Ephesians 6:10-17).

"…And having shod your feet with the preparation of the gospel of peace" (Ephesians 6:15). Who knew footwear was an essential part of warfare?

The answer—one of the greatest Kingdom warriors who ever lived, the apostle Paul. Battles have been won or lost in history because one side was better equipped, not with their weaponry, but with what they wore on their feet.

Once again, this makes a lot of sense when Paul tells us to put on the whole armor of God. Just like you plan your outward attire as you get dressed in the morning based on your anticipated activity for the day, we put on our footwear accordingly.

I've been called "a man of many shirts." I quit wearing suits while preaching only a couple of years into my ministry, even though in my faith tradition that was all I ever saw any pastor wear. A short time later, I was liberated from the worst invention ever imposed on the male gender—neckties! (Seriously, whoever thought cinching a fancy rope around our necks was a good idea?) I started preaching in slacks and a dress shirt before I finally gravitated to wearing jeans or occasionally nice pants or slacks.

I'll never forget several years ago when one of the teenage boys in our church came up to me after Sunday services and announced that he had won the family bet that day. Apparently, they had all taken a guess on the way to church that morning as to what I would be wearing. He said, "I guessed right. I knew you would be wearing your khaki slacks and maroon-colored shirt." It was right then and there I decided I had become way too predictable and needed to expand my wardrobe. Hence, I'm now "a man of many shirts."

What most would never guess is that my wife calls me "a man of many shoes." She is often after me to purge my collection of shoes, but I never do. I might only wear a pair once in a while, but they all have a different purpose. Some I have had for years, but I never know when I might need them again! I have dressy boots, cowboy boots, hiking boots, hunting boots, work boots, rubber boots, and even my old combat boots. I keep old tennis shoes for floating and fishing or doing yard work. I have newer athletic shoes for running and working out. I have a pair of "lifestyle" sneakers, Air Jordans, that just look cool besides being comfortable. I have several pairs of flip flops, but I'm not sure why. Then, of course, I have dress shoes in both black and brown that I wear on Sundays or when I'm wearing "business casual" to the office. One pair even has pointed toes. (A gift from my son-in-law who was probably attempting to keep me looking young, even though when I wear them my feet remind me I'm actually old.) I wear them anyway.

We choose our footwear based on our anticipated activity. I sometimes wear my black dress shoes with pointed toes when I preach on Sunday morning. But I wouldn't dream of hiking the Grand Canyon in them. I bought a pair of hiking boots specifically for that purpose. Paul is saying that if we anticipate going into battle, we will be careful to put on our spiritual combat boots every day. We always choose our shoes specifically for their intended purpose. Paul is reminding us that our chosen footwear is a critical part of our success in warfare. The *"gospel of peace"* is what we wear for war.

Shoes matter to a soldier. You need a sure footing and a sure foundation. Whether it was the day you were saved or when you wake up on Monday, your only sure footing is standing on the certainty and the sure foundation of the finished work of the Lord Jesus Christ.

Remember, the armor of a Roman soldier is a physical picture of the spiritual armor God has given us. As soldiers of the Lord and children of the living God, we are at war daily against principalities, powers, rulers of the darkness of this age, and spiritual hosts of wickedness in heavenly places. How are we to fight supernatural enemies? How are we to fight demonic powers and authorities? He's saying we better make sure we are wearing the right shoes.

Physically, a Roman soldier's shoes are a picture of our spiritual shoes, which Paul says must be the shoes of the gospel of peace.

We would not immediately consider the shoes of the soldier to be all that critical to his survival in combat—unlike the helmet, breastplate, sword, and shield. Those things are all obvious, but do shoes really matter? When you look throughout history, you discover that wars have been won or lost because one army had better footwear than the other.

Alexander the Great conquered the entire known world. One of the reasons he did is because he had 30,000 foot soldiers who were known to have the ability to move very quickly with speed, agility, mobility, and efficiency. They would cover huge amounts of territory in one day, quickly overtaking their enemy before they were battle ready—all because the soldiers wore a good pair of shoes.

Consider the United States Civil War. It is well known that many of the soldiers fighting on the side of the south went into battle barefoot. If one army has combat boots and the other side is fighting barefoot, which one do you think has an advantage? One army is able to move quickly and efficiently, and the other army has many soldiers with no protection on their feet. An army marches on its feet and fights on its feet. If you don't have strong feet, you are not going to be very strong in battle. Shoes are critical.

The gospel to us spiritually is what a Roman soldier's shoes were to him physically. A Roman soldier's shoes were for two things: standing and advancing. A soldier's shoes helped him stand against the onslaught of the enemy and advance against the enemy. It is the same for our shoes, the gospel of peace.

In warfare, there are times when you are standing and times you are advancing. We learn in spiritual warfare that the way we advance is to stand. Four times Paul reminds us of this very point in a few short verses. Remember, Jesus has taken the high ground already.

Just like a Roman soldier would have tied his shoes tightly and double-knotted them to be ready for battle, you had better make sure your shoes are secure and that *"your feet are fitted with the readiness that comes from the gospel of peace"* (Ephesians 6:15 NIV).

The Roman soldier had a very special and remarkable pair of shoes for battle. The soldiers would stand at the skirmish line with their shields, shoulder to shoulder, against the advance of the enemy. Picture hundreds of men running at you, throwing their weight against you. If you don't have shoes that can dig in against them, they're going to easily push you backward. It was the Romans who invented what we know today as cleats—shoes with dozens of spikes driven through the soles. They would use them to dig in and stand against the attack of the enemy and then to move quickly and advance on the enemy.

Paul says our spiritual shoes are the *"gospel of peace"* because they are a sure foundation. The gospel is all we need to "dig in" and stand against the enemy. Soccer players and football players use cleats today for the same reason—so they can dig in, make cuts quickly, and move with speed and agility. In the very same way, Roman soldiers would use cleated sandals because there were times they needed to stand and there were other times they needed to advance. If they didn't have spikes to help them dig in, they would have been slipping and sliding all over the battlefield.

You cannot stand against your enemy if you don't have on the sure foundation of the right pair of shoes. We use our shoes much more as a stylistic item today, but in Jesus' day, that wasn't necessarily the case. We can tell a lot about somebody today simply by looking at their shoes. You would never dream of wearing ballerina slippers to play a football game.

Here's the point: You cannot stand against the enemy unless you are standing on the gospel, the finished work of the Lord Jesus Christ.

You match your shoes with whatever you need them to do. You had better wear the right shoes to allow you to dig in and stand up against the enemy and the advance of the adversary so you're not slipping and sliding all over the place.

> We are to stand on the Lord's work and stand on His Word.

As mentioned previously, historically in warfare whoever has the high ground wins. Your goal is to fight from an elevated position. What Paul is saying four times is to dig in and stand. Don't give up the high ground. Stand firm on the work of the Son of God, the truth of the Word of God, and on Christ's victory over the enemy of our soul.

Paul reminds us that we never stand on what *we* do. We stand only on what *Christ* has done! When he says to *"shod your feet with the preparation of the gospel of peace,"* Paul is reminding us that Jesus has won the day. The gospel is our victory—the good news that Christ died for our sins and three days later He arose and is seated with our heavenly Father. All we have to do as we battle with the enemy is simply stand on what Christ has done at Calvary!

CHAPTER 10

JESUS WON THE DAY!

Having disarmed principalities and powers, He [Jesus] *made a public spectacle of them, triumphing over them in it* (Colossians 2:15).

There is nothing worse than your team losing the game and watching your opponents celebrate right in front of you. Yet that is exactly what Jesus did! When Christ came out of the grave, He cut down the nets and tore down the goalposts. In a manner of speaking, He did a touchdown dance in the end zone right in front of His enemies. I don't know what that looked like, but what I do know is Jesus celebrated the victory of the ages in the face of His enemies. He triumphed over them and made a public spectacle of them. In my mind, I see Him pointing in their face and saying, "You lose! I have won the day!" He might have even done a break dance or moonwalk out of the grave.

I have blood and sweat equity in the football program at the University of Kansas. Since I played there in the late eighties and early nineties, the football program has had its ups and downs with more down years than up. A few years ago, they were soaring with a run of really good years. Our archrivals from the University of Missouri had some really good teams too at about the same time. The two programs met for several years in a row for the Border War in Kansas City at Arrowhead Stadium, home of the Kansas City Chiefs. The media called it "Arrowhead Armageddon." Not quite, but they were really big games for both programs.

In one of the last games I went to in the iconic series played at Arrowhead Stadium, Mizzou beat my Jayhawks in the closing moments of the game. We lost on a last-second field goal. I will admit, I was heartbroken. Twenty years earlier, I had suited up for Kansas for moments like this. It was a tough loss. The worst part was the very long walk back to the car in the middle of ten thousand Missouri fans celebrating their victory and chanting one letter at a time, "M-I-Z, Z-O-U, M-I-Z, Z-O-U." (I remember wondering if it was because they were Missouri alums that they had to shorten "Missouri" to only six letters so they could all remember how to spell it.)

As painful as that memory may be, I share it because it sets the scene for what happened when Jesus came out of the grave. When Jesus came out of the grave, He could have been chanting one letter at a time "H-E-A-V-E-N," heaven has won the day! He had triumphed over them, and it's time for the winning side to rush the field of battle. The game is over, and we are on the winning side!

Here's the point: Jesus Christ has won the day so you can have victory every day.

You win every battle when you simply stand on the finished work of Jesus Christ—the blood of the Lamb—and the truth of the Word of God because Satan cannot undo the work that Christ has done. You don't have to do a thing because with Christ, everything has already been done. The victory has already been won. Just stand. That is our source of peace! That's why Paul calls it the *"gospel of peace."* He is saying we can have more than just peace *with* God. Even in the middle of the hottest battles of life, we can have the peace *of* God.

PEACE *WITH* GOD AND THE PEACE *OF* GOD

I'm amazed that right in the middle of his dissertation on warfare, the apostle Paul writes about peace: *"Having shod your feet with the preparation of the gospel of peace...."* He is convinced that we can have peace in the middle of this battle of the ages. He says even though we wrestle daily against principalities, powers, the rulers of the darkness of this age, and spiritual hosts of wickedness in the heavenly places, we can still have a sense of peace. I am convinced that every human being, and perhaps the entire world, longs for rest rather than war.

> And the peace of God, which surpasses all understanding,
> will guard your hearts and minds through Christ Jesus
> (Philippians 4:7).

Creation has never been at rest. Since the fall of Lucifer, when he rebelled against God in an attempt to usurp the throne of God, he has been waging war, and the casualty of this warfare is all of creation.

Romans 8:22 tells us, *"For we know that the whole creation groans and labors with birth pangs together until now."* In other words, all of creation groans under the weight of sin and travails under the curse of sin. Rest is always the work of the One we can rest in whose name is Jesus, but warfare is the work of rebellion. It was Lucifer's rebellion that brought warfare to the heavenlies; it was Adam's rebellion that brought warfare to the earth.

This world is not the world God created. His was a world of perfection—free from pain, death, and destruction. The moment sin entered creation it erased God's perfection, and the world we now live in is the result of the curse of sin. It's a world at war with itself and with God. All the wars, bloodshed, death, diseases, natural disasters, cataclysms, and chaos are because of the curse of sin. It's because of sin that we live in a world of pain instead of peace, a world of suffering instead of joy, and a world under travail instead of tranquility.

One day God's perfection will return to creation, and we will indeed have peace on earth. But there can be no peace on earth until the Prince of Peace comes back to the earth. When Christ returns at the Second Coming, the curse of sin is going to be lifted. The beautiful story of God is that paradise lost is one day going to be paradise restored. Even so, come quickly Lord Jesus! Until that day, Paul is assuring us that we can have rest in the middle of this warfare, even now.

Here's the point: We can have peace that goes beyond all understanding in the middle of a world full of pain.

Paul calls it the gospel of peace because apart from Christ, you are not at peace with God. Apart from Christ, the Bible tells us we're at war with God, estranged and separated from Him.

The Bible says in John 3:16, *"For God so loved the world...."* God loves you apart from Christ in that He loves all people. He has a universal love for everybody in the world, but if you are not in Christ, you are apart from Christ. God may love you in the universal sense that He loves all people, but apart from Christ you're not a child of God, and He doesn't have a wonderful plan for your life. You're estranged from God and an enemy of God. Apart from Christ, there is no rest, there's only war.

For the wrath of God is revealed from heaven against all ungodliness and unrighteousness of men… (Romans 1:18).

The NIV puts it this way: *"The wrath of God is being revealed from heaven against all the godlessness and wickedness of people, who suppress the truth by their wickedness"* (Romans 1:18). The righteousness of God demands a penalty and punishment for sin. When we come into the world physically, we are not at peace with God. In fact, there is enmity between God and us.

Christ died for one reason—to make peace with God for you.

Here's the amazing thing about the redemptive plan of God— He loved us so much that He poured out His wrath upon His sinless Son instead of us. It pleased God to crush His own Son on the cross of Calvary—the eternal, sinless, Son of God—rather than crush you. Christ died for one reason, and that is to make peace with God for you.

CHAPTER 11

CHRIST OUR PEACE

But now in Christ Jesus you who once were far off have been brought near by the blood of Christ. For He Himself is our peace, who has made both one, and has broken down the middle wall of separation (Ephesians 2:13-14).

Paul says that at one time, you were estranged from God and far from Him. You could not draw near to Him. The blood of Christ is God's peace offering for sin. It's the blood of Christ that has torn down the wall of sin between God and humankind. God's redemptive plan is to make peace with God and all people. There had to be somebody who would offer a sacrifice, somebody who would bear the penalty of sin. So that's exactly what God did. He has made peace with us through the blood of the Son of God.

And by Him to reconcile all things to Himself, by Him,
whether things on earth or things in heaven, having made
peace through the blood of His cross (Colossians 1:20).

Jesus came *"to reconcile all things to Himself."* That is the essence of the gospel of peace. God's plan to bring peace between Himself and humanity was to offer His Son upon the cross of Calvary, and He accomplished that through the gospel of Jesus Christ. The gospel of Jesus Christ is that He died for our sin, He was buried—but three days later He rose from the dead, and He is alive forevermore.

You sometimes hear about a husband and wife who are divorced or separated, and then they get back together. We say they are reconciled. That's what God did for us through the gospel. We were estranged from God and separated from Him as His enemies. We were divorced from Him, but because of the blood of the Son of God, we can now be reconciled to Him. He has made a peace offering through the blood; He offers peace with Him instead of separation and sin.

This scarlet thread is woven throughout all sixty-six books of the Bible. Consider the book of Leviticus that tells us about the five offerings of the ancient Hebrews. The ancient Jews would bring five sacrificial offerings that God used over and over again throughout the centuries as a prophetic picture of what Christ would do on the cross of Calvary. They would bring a lamb or a ram to the altar in the courtyard of the tabernacle. It couldn't be just any lamb; it had to be one without spot or blemish. Many people think Leviticus is a morbid book because of all the sacrifices and blood. God used the sacrifices to prophetically paint a picture, centuries in advance, of the one final sacrifice, the Lamb of God who was without spot or blemish.

In the Old Testament book of Leviticus, God established the wilderness tabernacle and instituted five offerings. The first three were the burnt offering, the meal offering, and the peace offering. Then came the trespass offering and the sin offering. All five offerings represented what God promised to do for His people when He offered up the Lamb of God on the cross of Calvary. God's truly amazing, ingenious mind placed these offerings in a very specific order. The burnt offering came first, then the meal offering, and then the peace offering.

The burnt offering pictured total consecration in that it was the only offering completely consumed upon the altar. It was burned in the fire and reduced to ash. It was a prophetic portrait of Jesus on the cross, completely consumed for our sins. The ancient Hebrews would take a pure, spotless male lamb, slay it on the altar spilling its blood, and then have it completely consumed in the fire of the brazen altar. This is exactly what Jesus Christ would become for us as He offered up His life on the cross of Calvary. He held nothing back—He gave all He had. He would shed His blood, and the fire of God's wrath would fall upon Him instead of you and me.

Next was the meal offering. It was the only bloodless offering because it did not speak of Christ's death but rather His spotless, sinless life. Instead of offering a blood offering, the people of God would make an offering of fine unleavened flour or meal. Leaven in the Bible is a picture of sin and speaks of Jesus as the unleavened *"bread of life"* (John 6:48). The Jews would bring unleavened meal or flour from which they would make bread as a prophetic picture of the sinless life of our Lord Jesus Christ. It had to be a sinless sacrifice. Had Jesus sinned even one time, He could not have been our sacrifice for sin.

Then came the third offering, which was the peace offering. Whereas the burnt offering had to be a male lamb representing Jesus Christ as the male Lamb of God, the peace offering could be male or female—not coincidental but completely providential!

Jesus has brought peace to all men and all women!

Isn't God amazing? Because Jesus gave His life (burnt offering), after having lived a sinless life (meal offering), we now have peace with God (peace offering). Jesus became our burnt offering by giving Himself completely as He was consumed in the fire of God's wrath, spilling His own blood. He was our meal offering. He couldn't have been the burnt offering had He not lived an unleavened life. Because He was a spotless, sinless sacrifice, He could become our peace offering before God. When you anchor your faith in the sacrifice of the Lord Jesus Christ, you immediately have peace with God.

Therefore, having been justified by faith, we have peace with God through our Lord Jesus Christ (Romans 5:1).

We are no longer at war with God, and we are now one with Him because Christ is our peace. The blood of Christ has torn down the walls of sin and separation between God and humankind, and He has become the peace offering.

Think about it. When a husband and wife have a disagreement, usually it's the offending party who has to make the peace offering. The amazing thing about God is that we are the offending party, yet we had nothing we could offer God. There is nothing we have that He needed or wanted. There is nothing we can offer to make peace between us. Because of His love for us, He made the peace offering for us. He's the One who took the punishment and paid the penalty even though we were the offending party, and we were guilty.

Are you constantly wondering, *Am I going to get to heaven? Will God accept me when I get there? Does God still love me?* You are really not sure if you died today where you would be or what you would see if you opened your eyes in eternity. You have no peace because you don't know with certainty your eternal destiny. Paul is trying to tell you the reason. It's because you are wearing the wrong pair of shoes— you're not standing on the gospel. You are standing on what *you* do instead of standing exclusively on what *Jesus* has done for you.

Stand firm on the gospel of peace.

Here's the point: Until you are standing on the gospel of peace, with your feet fitted with the preparation of the gospel of peace, you will forever be a pushover for the adversary.

Ephesians 6:15 (AMP) says it this way:

> *...And having strapped on your feet the gospel of peace in preparation [to face the enemy with firm-footed stability and the readiness produced by the good news].*

Satan knows you are standing on shaky ground instead of the solid ground of Jesus. Until you stop working to appease God, you will never have the peace of God. Satan knows this all too well, and he will use your efforts to appease God against you every time.

CHAPTER 12

GOD'S AMAZING GRACE

For by grace you have been saved through faith, and that not of yourselves; it is the gift of God, not of works, lest anyone should boast (Ephesians 2:8-9).

You may be like the average American, trying to appease God by the things you do instead of simply trusting in what God has done for you. When you ask people if they know for sure they are going to heaven, many say, "Well, I don't know for sure if I'm going to heaven, I think I'm going to heaven. I mean, I'm a pretty good person, and I've tried to do the right things, but I don't think anybody can know for sure if they're going to heaven. I mean how do you know if you have done enough?"

In essence, what they are saying is they hope they have appeased God by doing enough good things, but they don't really have the peace of God and can't say with certainty they are going to heaven.

You will never get to heaven based on anything you do for God; you only get to heaven by putting your faith in what God has already done for you. Paul says in Ephesians 2:8-9 that we are saved by grace, through faith, plus nothing. Nada, zilch! You cannot add one thing to what Christ has already done.

You are saved by grace through faith. What does that mean?

I like to explain grace like this. Years ago when I was a member of the police department, every once in a while, I would pull somebody over for blowing through a stop sign or red light. You wanted to get pulled over by me because there was a good chance that unless I had to write you a ticket, I wasn't going to write you a ticket. I gave you a warning if I could. You blew the stop sign, you blew the red light. You were guilty of breaking the law, and you deserved a penalty for breaking the law. If I withheld the penalty from you, even though you were guilty, I showed you grace.

That's what God did for us. We broke His law—that's called sin. We went through a stop sign where God was saying, "Stop, don't proceed." Because we blew through that stop sign, we are guilty of breaking the law, and we are guilty of sin. That meant we were guilty of the penalty, and we deserved the punishment. But God withheld the penalty. He withheld from us the punishment and did one better—He paid the penalty instead. That is grace! *"For by grace you have been saved through faith."*

Paul calls it a gift in Ephesians 2:9, it is *"not of works, lest anyone should boast."* A gift is something you get for free. If you have to earn it, it's not a gift, it's a reward. Heaven is not a reward for the righteous; it is a gift for the guilty. You receive this free gift of salvation when you put your faith and trust in the gracious act God accomplished on the cross of Calvary and God forgives you and restores you. No one gives their kids gifts at Christmas and then asks them to pay them back in January. You are giving it to them for free—they can't pay you for it.

There is nothing you can do that is going to get you into heaven. Your entrance into heaven can only be a result of your acknowledgment of what God has done for you. Titus 3:5 says, *"Not by works of righteousness which we have done, but according to His mercy He saved us...."* As long as you try to appease God by the things you do for Him, you will never have peace with God.

In Ephesians 6, Paul is writing about the peace with God that comes from standing on the finished work of Jesus Christ. Christ died for our sin, He was buried, three days later He rose from the dead, and He's alive forevermore. He's our peace offering; He has made peace with God for us. Now we simply stand on what Christ has done.

SHAKY GROUND

No matter how righteous or religious you think you are, no matter how moral or good or nice you might be, if you are standing on your work, you are standing on shaky ground because you have sinned and so have I. Some may say, "But I've been baptized." Yes, I'm glad you have, and I hope that you have been, but baptism is a ceremony. It's a ritual, a work that you do. I could sprinkle you or dunk you so many times you would turn into a prune, but it will not get you to heaven for even one day.

Others say, "I pray, I take communion, I go to church." Those are things *you* do—but you get to heaven based only on what *Christ* has done for you. I could put a wafer in your mouth, and you could drink from a shiny cup every day for the rest of your life. You could take communion every single hour of every single day, but you will not get to heaven based on anything you do for God. You get to heaven based only on what God has done for you, not by works of righteousness we have done. Christ alone is our peace. Peace with God comes by standing on the finished work of the Son of God.

Here's the point: Until you trust absolutely and exclusively in the finished work of the Son of God, you will never have any sense of peace with God. You'll just work and wonder, *Does God still love me? I wonder if He will accept me and if I've done enough to get into heaven.*

All Christians are saved by grace through faith. There is nothing you can do to earn your salvation because it's by grace alone through faith alone. However, you may have been taught that you have to work to hang on to your salvation, and if you sin too many times, you may lose it. You are constantly wondering where you stand with God. Ephesians 2:8-9 applies to how you are saved and how you stay saved: *"For by grace you have been saved through faith...."*

If I had to work to get my salvation, I would have never received my salvation. If it was my work to keep my salvation, I would have already lost my salvation. I don't just have peace *with* God but also the peace *of* God because I'm not trusting in any of my work to *be* saved or any of my work to *stay* saved.

Satan has stolen the peace of God from many Christians who believe the lie that they stay saved by their works. You may know with certainty your destiny eternally, but you lack peace. When the enemy is coming against you, and the Bible says that's exactly what happens daily, instead of standing against the enemy and simply digging in and saying, "I'm going to stand on the Word of God and the finished work of the Son of God," you immediately begin to retreat.

Satan comes to steal your joy. Jesus says in John 10:10 that the devil is a thief who comes to steal, kill, and destroy. He doesn't have to destroy your body because it's doomed to dust. He cannot war against your spirit because it has been sealed by God's Spirit; he cannot destroy your peace with God because it's based on the work of the Son of God, but he wants to destroy the peace *of* God. Satan is a thief that comes to steal your joy.

MENTAL WARFARE

Satan wars against the soul, which is our mind and emotions. Remember, I addressed this earlier, and I'm going to repeat it again and again. The warfare is taking place in your mind. Satan wants to control you by going on a mental campaign of doubt, discouragement, disillusion, dejection, and depression. It's mental warfare of the highest order.

Satan's warfare is not a physical conflict—it's spiritual and mental. If you read my first book, *Defeating the Enemy*, you know that he comes against us the very same way he came against Eve with one question: "Has God indeed said…?" He launches his attack through doubt. The moment he gets you to doubt what God has said, you are immediately in retreat. Instead of standing fast on what God has said in His Word, you start to doubt. When you doubt, you are backing up and giving ground to the enemy.

Many Christians doubt the work of God and doubt the Son of God when they face trials or tribulations or adverse situations. As a result, they lose their footing on the high ground. Remember, everything the enemy does is for one purpose: to take back ground that Christ has already given you. Those who take the most ground win the battle.

Ephesians 4:27 says not to give the devil a foothold. That old serpent has lost his place in your life, and he is relentless in his attempts to make you back up and retreat. All it takes is one false step backward to give him an opportunity to take back ground from you by controlling you with negative thoughts and emotions. It can happen so easily and quickly, almost unwittingly, and we don't even know it is happening.

It happened to me when I was working in the yard on a really windy day. I was near a tree, and all of a sudden, I was knocked silly. A limb came crashing down and hit me right on the head. I blacked out, and when I came to, my head and my face were covered in blood. My daughter was the first to see me as I walked in the house, dripping blood all over the floor. Her eyes were as big as saucers as she asked, "What happened to you? Is that a deadly wound?" Just as sincere as she could be, she said, "Are you going to live?"

As the emergency room doctor was stitching my head wound, he commented, "I may have left a piece of that limb or some bark in there." I didn't think it really happened, but I instantly had a lump on my head. To top it off, I had a flare-up of gout. I hadn't had a flare-up for a long time, but when I do, it's very debilitating and I can barely walk. I was literally a mess from the top of my head to the bottom of my feet. Needless to say, my week got off to a bad start, and I was in a bad mood all week long.

Mentally, I didn't even know what was happening. I just couldn't do what I needed to do. I couldn't be a good father, husband, leader, pastor, or preacher. If you are down mentally, if you have given ground to the enemy, you cannot function and live in victory.

Now it was Wednesday, and Sunday was coming. I was sitting at my computer, and I had nothing. I don't know what stress is in your life, but that is real stress for me. My weeks always begin the same way: Monday morning, "God, I have nothing." By Wednesday, I hope to have something. If I have nothing on Wednesday, I have stress. Then I realized what happened. I had given ground to the enemy, and I couldn't think clearly. I was distracted, easily diverted, and weighed down with doubt and discouragement.

It can happen in such a way that it's totally unwitting. Suddenly, we are giving up ground where God has given us victory. In warfare, it's all about taking ground. I was down that week for various reasons. I was feeling the stress. When we get squeezed, we have stress. We all have it, and we all live it because we are all made of the same stuff. You have stuff…I have stuff.

It's not a sin when you're down, but it IS a sin to stay down. Satan doesn't just want to get you down; he wants to give you such a sucker punch that you stay down and never get up again. The longer you stay down, the more ground you give up, and the more difficult it becomes to get up.

How do you regain the high ground? You do what Paul writes in Ephesians 6, you *"Stand!"*

Stand on the promise Jesus made when He said, *"The gates of Hades shall not prevail."* You declare, "I'm not going to give up this ground any longer. Satan, you have no authority; you have no victory. This is God's ground, this is His place of authority, and this is His victory."

Victory is your true identity regardless of whether or not it's your immediate reality.

Get this down in your spirit—victory is your true identity regardless of whether or not it's your immediate reality. Satan wants to steal your joy, and there are times in life that are not joyful. But your joy doesn't hinge on circumstances or situations or adverse tribulations. Your joy depends on one Person—Jesus. Satan cannot take that from you, and because he cannot take Jesus from you, he cannot steal your joy. You have to give it to him, and he had my joy during that week from hell.

Nehemiah 8:10 says, *"The joy of the Lord is your strength."* I had no strength; I had no sense of victory. It was not my immediate reality. When you begin to stand on the finished work of the Son of God and the absolute truth of the Word of God, you take back the ground you lost.

The truth of the Word of God in Second Corinthians 2:14 is that He *"always leads us in triumph in Christ."* Romans 8:37 tells us, *"In all of these things we are more than conquerors through Him who loved us."* First Corinthians 15:57 assures us that God *"gives us the victory through our Lord Jesus Christ."* And Jesus says in John 10:10, *"I have come that they* [you and I] *may have life, and that they may have it more abundantly."*

This is how you begin to stand up and take ground back from the enemy. Tell him: Satan, you have no authority over me because this is God's ground. I'm a blood-bought child of the King, of God Almighty. I have been ransomed and redeemed, and Jesus has set me free. Christ has secured my victory. He came to give me life abundantly, and I can live triumphantly even in the face of tragedy. Satan, you have no authority. You are not going to steal my joy; you are not going to control my thoughts or my emotions. I'm going to stand on what God has said. I'm going to stand on this ground that God has given. Jesus is my Lord and Savior.

You stand on what God has said regardless of what you see because there are times when what you see is different from what God has said. Trials, tribulations, and adverse situations are what the enemy wants you to see, but that is not your ultimate reality. Your ultimate reality, your ultimate identity is what God has said regardless of what you see.

Christ has secured our victory.

It is spiritual warfare. There are too many times we give ground to the enemy where Christ has already won the victory. Suit up with the whole armor of God, and don't give up ground when Christ has won the victory.

This is how you win, and this is how you take ground from the enemy. This is how you can find rest in the middle of the war. You simply rest in the work of the Son of God and in the facts of the Word of God. You stand fast!

> *For shoes, put on the peace that comes from the Good News so that you will be fully prepared* (Ephesians 6:15 NLT).

PART VI

YOUR SHIELD OF FAITH ON LIFE'S BATTLEFIELD

Finally, my brethren, be strong in the Lord and in the power of His might. Put on the whole armor of God, that you may be able to stand against the wiles of the devil. For we do not wrestle against flesh and blood, but against principalities, against powers, against the rulers of the darkness of this age, against spiritual hosts of wickedness in the heavenly places. Therefore take up the whole armor of God, that you may be able to withstand in the evil day, and having done all, to stand. Stand therefore, having girded your waist with truth, having put on the breastplate of righteousness, and having shod your feet with the preparation of the gospel of peace; above all, taking the shield of faith with which you will be able to quench all the fiery darts of the wicked one. And take the helmet of salvation, and the sword of the Spirit, which is the word of God (Ephesians 6:10-17).

In warfare, how does the military "soften up" the fortifications of the enemy? Today it's with air raids and heavy artillery. For several days before the Allied forces landed on the beaches of Normandy, Allied battleships bombarded Nazi fortifications. In 1991, when President George H.W. Bush sent American troops into Kuwait to liberate it from a maniacal Iraqi dictator named Saddam Hussein, the assault did not begin with ground troops. It began with what he called the "shock and awe" of thousands of powerful bombs being dropped from the sky by a coalition of warplanes along with hundreds of laser-guided missiles launched into Iraqi fortifications.

In the ancient world, long before modern technology and mechanized warfare, armies would soften up the enemy lines through a barrage of flaming arrows. This is what Paul has in view when he says in Ephesians 6:16, *"Above all, taking the shield of faith with which you will be able to quench the fiery darts of the wicked one."*

We have been learning how, as the Church of Jesus Christ, we can take ground from the enemy, advance against our adversary, and live in victory. We're taking each piece of our armor and learning how God has equipped us for spiritual warfare so we can live in victory against all the power of the enemy. In verse 16, Paul tells us that the shield is perhaps more important than any other piece of the armor. He says, *"above all."* In other words, even more importantly than what we've already learned about, *"above all, taking the shield of faith with which you will be able to quench all the fiery darts of the wicked one."*

We live in a society that increasingly does not view the world through a lens of good and evil, light and darkness, right and wrong. Rather, the mantra of our day is, "Is there really any such thing as good and evil? Who's to say who's right and who's wrong? One person's terrorist is another person's freedom fighter." You read or hear people say that kind of thing often. The concept of good being at war with evil repels a lot of people.

The Bible describes not only a world that is at war but a universe that has been at war since the moment Lucifer rebelled against God. Like it or not, we are part of that war because good *is* at war with evil. Two kingdoms are colliding—Light versus darkness.

If you have been born again by faith in Jesus Christ, you are no longer part of the kingdom of darkness. You have a new Kingdom and a new King, and His name is Jesus. As children of the Light, God is teaching us through the pen of the apostle Paul how to wage war against the darkness of our world—against principalities, powers, the rulers of the darkness—the fallen angels under Satan's control.

In ancient warfare, it was common for an army to have hundreds or even thousands of archers. It was also common to soften up your enemy before sending in the infantry. With archers standing back about 200-300 yards, they would launch a surge of hundreds of arrows at their enemy as they were advancing. Often, those archers would dip their arrows in pitch and light them on fire before launching them into the enemy.

Just imagine that as you are advancing on your enemy, you look up to see a wall of fire falling from the sky, coming at you. It would have been the ancient equivalent of napalm. It was a double threat because not only would the arrows penetrate whatever they hit, but potentially fire could spread throughout an entire battalion of soldiers, creating chaos and pandemonium that would cause them to break formation. Militarily, it was a genuine threat.

Before the Roman soldiers would go into battle, they would wrap their shields in layers of leather and soak them in water. When they went into battle and the enemy launched a barrage of flaming arrows, they were able to take cover behind their shields. When those flaming arrows hit their shields, not only would they be protected from the arrows, but because they had been drenched and soaked in water, the flames would be quenched as well.

Spiritually, these flaming arrows or fiery darts illustrate the bombardment of our minds by the enemy in our thoughts, impressions, imaginations, impulsions, and emotions. These flaming arrows from the enemy are always lies he launches against us. Physically, these flaming arrows are a picture of what happens mentally as Satan attempts to "soften up" the fortified position we have in Christ.

THE BATTLEGROUND

Remember, the battleground is always in the mind. Satan does not have to destroy our bodies; they are already destined to be destroyed under Adam's curse. He cannot destroy our spirit once we have been born again of God's Spirit. The salvation of our spirit is sealed by God's Spirit (Ephesians 1:13, 4:30). Satan primarily targets our soul—the mind, the will, and the emotions. The battleground is always what takes place between our ears.

> The battleground takes place between our ears.

In the spiritual realm, Satan releases a bombardment of flaming arrows, one after another, targeting our mind and emotions—ungodly thoughts or negative emotions—as he wars against our soul. He targets the soul because that is the control center of the human being, and whoever or whatever controls your soul, your mind, and emotions controls you.

The flaming arrows he tries to hit us with are as varied as we are individually. Fear and intimidation are certainly at the top of the list of arrows that he shoots in an attempt to control us. Remember, he's a roaring lion (First Peter 5:8), and he seeks to intimidate you and hold you in fear. Sometimes it's obvious; sometimes it's more subtle.

I will never forget the night the church I now pastor voted me in. When I went to bed, I was no longer a cop; I was now a pastor. I woke up in the middle of the night, and there was an evil, demonic presence in my bedroom. I'm not scared by very many things in life, but I was instantly petrified. It sounded like a freight train running through the middle of my bedroom. Secular psychologists would say I was just having an anxiety attack or a panic attack. They only recognize the psychological factors. They don't understand that we are also spiritual.

Yes, I was under a lot of anxiety because I was leaving the predictability and the paycheck of the only career I had ever known. I was burning that bridge; on paper, there was no reason to think I could succeed in the ministry. After all, I was a cop. I knew how to serve an arrest warrant, how to clear a gang of drug dealers off the street corner, and how to quell a riot. But I didn't know how to be a pastor. I had never been to pastor school, I had never been in the ministry, and I had very little formal training. In March 2000, I quite literally went to bed a cop and woke up a pastor, and it didn't come without an element of fear—fear of the future, fear of failure, fear of the unknown.

That uncertainty was all Satan needed, and he knew exactly how to strike. One of his emissaries came to me that night for no other reason than to intimidate me and strike fear of failure in me. When I woke up, the first words out of my mouth were, "My God, what have I done?" It was like waking up from a dream, only to realize it wasn't a dream. Suddenly I realized it was all too real. Instantly I was awake and terrified as I thought, *My God, what have I done! I said yes! I'm now a pastor, and there's no going back!* Panic!

I began to call on Jesus, and I went back to sleep and that was it. It was over. It has only happened one other time in my life. It was right after I released my first book, *Defeating the Enemy,* and I was preaching through the chapters of the book on Sunday mornings. I woke up in the middle of the night, and instantly I was in a panic again. I was terrified. This time I said, "I'm not scared of you. I'm under the blood of the Lamb." And that was it. It was over. I don't know why it happened. There are times when Satan comes in such a way that you know exactly who it is, and you know exactly what it is. There was no doubt in my mind there was a demonic presence in my bedroom.

Most of the time in our lives the devil's tactics are far more subtle because he doesn't always come as a roaring lion. Instead, he comes as an angel of light. He wants to blend in. He doesn't want you to know he's there, so he lurks below the surface launching subtle fiery darts of fear, intimidation, depression, or discouragement.

In First Samuel 16, King Saul was given a demonic spirit, but several times in the Bible it's called a "distressing spirit." It was sent to Saul for one reason—to discourage, distress, and depress him. Today, King Saul would probably be diagnosed with clinical depression. That is why secular psychology falls woefully short. Secular psychology only looks at the psychological factors; it does not recognize there are also spiritual factors. Far too often only the symptom is treated instead of dealing with the root of the problem. King Saul struggled with depression, but his problem was not a clinical condition—his problem was a demonic spirit that had been sent to him. I know because

I battle this spirit. Every Monday, I have to stand my ground and not give up the high ground. I have to purposely raise my shield of faith.

DIVERTING EMOTIONAL ARROWS

The devil will make you a target, shooting emotional arrows of fear, intimidation, depression, discouragement, anger, bitterness, and unforgiveness as well as envy, jealousy, lust, loneliness, guilt, greed, and pride. Remember, the devil is not omniscient like God. He cannot read your mind or your thoughts, but he desires to plant a thought inside your mind and then convince you his thoughts are your thoughts. His desire is to control your thoughts and then control your emotions. His purpose is to give you that thought or trigger some emotion for no other reason than to control, discourage, tempt, and afflict you.

Any ungodly thought, impulse, or emotion that will potentially draw you away from God or draw you away from oneness with God is a flaming arrow of the adversary. He wants to stop you, hinder you, discourage you, and ultimately destroy you. He might manipulate people in your life, or he might manipulate circumstances or situations in your life to trigger any of these ungodly thoughts, impulses, or emotions.

The enemy might attack your life externally, but his real desire is to control you internally. In other words, he might attack you through your physical health or your material wealth. He might attack you through your family, or he might attack you relationally. But ultimately he is targeting and attacking your soul—the mind, will, and emotions—through your thoughts and your emotions.

Satan hunts like a lion, which means he studies his prey. He knows you, and he knows which buttons to push in your life. He knows how to target you. He knows your weaknesses, your insecurities, your fears, and he knows exactly how to craft an arrow specifically for you. For some people, it's bitterness, and he'll shoot a barrage of bitterness arrows against them. For other people, it's guilt, and he shoots one guilty arrow after another at his target. For somebody else, it may be arrows of rejection or lust. Whatever it is, Satan knows how to target you. He knows where the bull's-eye is on you. Everybody has a bull's-eye, and he crafts his arrows specifically for you.

Thankfully, you have the shield of faith that saves you from anything the devil can devise.

CHAPTER 13

FIGHTING THE GOOD FIGHT OF FAITH

Fight the good fight of faith, lay hold on eternal life, to which you were also called and have confessed the good confession in the presence of many witnesses (1 Timothy 6:12).

The question is, how do we combat and quench the fiery darts of the enemy? Paul tells us in Ephesians 6:16, *"Above all, taking the shield of faith with which you will be able to quench all the fiery darts of the wicked one."* In other words, faith is our shield, and when you are under a barrage of ungodly thoughts or ungodly emotions, you need to raise your shield of faith. Faith is believing what God has said, regardless of what you see. It's trusting in the truth of God's Word over anything you may feel.

165

That means when you are under a bombardment of enemy lies and he's assaulting your mind with thoughts or emotions that want to control you, you have to immediately go to God's Word, throw up your shield, and put your faith in what God has said regardless of what you see. It means believing the truth of God's Word regardless of what you feel. That is the problem for a lot of people.

Satan knows we are emotionally driven beings, and he wants to control our emotions because most people will obey their emotions. You've heard of being an emotional "basket case," and there's a reason Satan wants you to be that way. You cannot trust your feelings exclusively because they sometimes lie. Your feelings are often tied to your flesh, your fallen nature, so you have to get to the point in life where you let God's Word define your ultimate reality. Your ultimate reality is not what you are feeling. Your ultimate reality is not even what you are thinking. Your ultimate reality is what God has said.

If I feel fearful, I need to throw up my shield of faith. Second Timothy 1:7 says, *"For God has not given us a spirit of fear, but of power...."* I will not live in fear because God has given me a spirit of power.

If I'm feeling anxious and anxiety is overcoming me, I need to raise my shield of faith. Philippians 4:6-7 says:

> **Be anxious for nothing**, *but in everything by prayer and supplication, with thanksgiving, let your requests be made known to God; and* **the peace of God**, *which surpasses all understanding,* **will guard your hearts and minds** *through Christ Jesus.*

I will not be anxious; I'm going to take my anxiety to God because He has promised to take care of me.

If Satan is shooting flaming arrows of doubt that say, "God can't take care of you, you are in way too deep this time, there is no hope for you," I need to raise my shield of faith. Philippians 4:19 tells us, *"And my God shall supply all your need according to His riches in glory by Christ Jesus."* Satan, you are a liar; you are a deceiver. God has said He will provide for me, and I'm going to believe what God has said regardless of what I see.

Raise the shield of faith when you are tempted to sin and your flesh is screaming, "I have to give in" and Satan is whispering, "You might as well just give in." What has God said? Romans 6:6-7 says that *"our old* [sin nature] *was crucified with Him, that the body of sin might be done away with, that we should no longer be slaves of sin. For he who has died has been freed from sin."*

God's Word says I am free from sin! I don't have to sin. I don't have to cave in to temptation no matter what Satan says. Satan, you are a liar and a deceiver. I don't have to give in to sin because I'm born again!

Lift up the shield of faith, and determine to believe the facts of God's Word regardless of what you see or feel. The instant you realize there's a barrage of enemy lies coming against you through emotions or thoughts, you have to choose immediately to throw up your shield and put your faith in what God has said. Your ultimate reality must be defined by what God has said regardless of what you think, feel, or see.

Faith is being fully persuaded that God will do what He says He will do, even when we can't see it (Romans 4:21). The best definition of faith I have heard is: "Faith is believing something is so when it isn't so, so it will be so because God said it's so." Faith isn't believing in whatever I want, and if I believe it enough I can get it. No, that's not what faith is. Faith is always anchored in God's Word. Jesus and God's Word must be the object of your faith. Faith is acting like something is so when it isn't so, so it will be so because God said it's so. It's simply taking God at His Word. What God has said, He will do!

Faith is always anchored in God's Word.

Practically, that means when I feel overwhelmed with a trial or tribulation and I don't know if I can carry this cross any longer or make it another day because the weight of this cross is so heavy, I raise my shield of faith—the Word of God. Philippians 4:13 says, *"I can do all things through Christ who strengthens me."* What I know is that right now I don't feel I can do it. I don't feel I have any hope in this, but God says, *"I can do all things through Christ who strengthens me."* I'm going to act like I can because God says I can.

Here's the point: Faith is action, not merely emotion.

Make the decision that you're not going to live like a victim when you belong to the Victor. You're not going to live defeated when you can live dynamically. Whether you're facing cancer, a family crisis, or financial cataclysm, lift up your shield of faith.

Romans 8:37 says, *"Yet in all these things we are more than conquerors...."* Maybe you don't feel very much like a conqueror right now, but God says you are *more* than a conqueror, so make the decision to believe what God has said regardless of what you feel.

In the ancient world, a warrior's shield was a piece of his defensive armory. It protected him from the weapons of the enemy that all had sharp points on the end. In hand-to-hand combat, his shield was not only part of his defensive equipment, but it also became an offensive weapon that often had a foot-long spike in the center of it. Imagine how lethal that shield would become in close-quarters combat when the warrior beat back his enemy with his shield.

Choose not to live like a victim—you belong to the Victor!

There are times when the enemy will come in for a close-quarters assault after trying to soften up the fortified positions of your mind. "I'm going through this horrible time of suffering, Phil. You don't understand what I'm going through. I've been suffering for so long. It seems like God isn't there, or He doesn't care." Raise your shield and start swinging at the enemy! Jesus said, *"In the world you will have tribulation,"* yes, you will, *"but be of good cheer, I have overcome the world"* (John 16:33). That means even when you suffer, you can be an overcomer because Christ suffered, and He overcame even death itself.

So the question is this: Will I be controlled by my emotions and my flesh, or will I be submitted to what God has said and the truth of His Word? That is how you fight with the shield of faith.

The moment that barrage of enemy arrows assaults you, you have a choice to make. Who will you believe? Jesus said Satan is a liar in John 8:44 and *"there is no truth in him...he is a liar and the father of it."* Satan, you are a liar, but the voice of truth is the Word of God. I'm going to believe what God has said, regardless of what I see or feel. That is how you defeat the enemy with the shield of faith.

When you are under a deluge of enemy lies, even though you may know they're not true intellectually and you understand it's irrational, it can feel very much like reality. I know sometimes it's not as easy as it sounds. Let me share with you something that happened to me not long ago that will help you in your fight of faith.

NEVER FIGHT ALONE

Satan not only knows your weaknesses, but he knows your strengths. There are times he actually will strike at your strength. My strength is the spiritual gift of prophecy. It's a supernatural ability to proclaim God's revelation with power and authority. Those of us with the gift of prophecy quickly see truth from error, right from wrong, and black from white in this world full of dingy "gray."

One of the things those with the gift of prophecy value most is integrity and authenticity. We hate hypocrisy, and we hate it most of all in our own lives. Satan knows that about me. A few years ago, my church was having what we called a revival week. I preached on strongholds Sunday through Wednesday, and we were in hot pursuit of Satan's territory. People were delivered that week from sin and bondage, and we were trying to help people biblically to overcome those life-controlling issues.

From the age of 21, I have pursued integrity and walked in integrity. I am the same person publicly that I am privately. I have nothing to hide from anybody. But something happened to me that weekend that had never happened before and has never happened since. I came under a bombardment of Satan's flaming arrows like I had never been through in my life. I was utterly convinced I was the biggest hypocrite who ever walked into the church.

Satan knows my mind like he knows your mind. I'm going to tell you about my mind, and I think it's probably true of your mind. If I'm not crucifying my mind daily and putting on the helmet of salvation, which I'll share with you in the next chapter, my thoughts can go from godly to ungodly in a fraction of a second. If I'm not consecrating my thoughts daily, my carnal, fallen mind can run away with thoughts that are unclean and ungodly! Satan knows that, and he leverages that against me from time to time.

All weekend long, I was under a flurry of flaming arrows. I felt guilty about sins I had never even committed because I knew I could have. I was feeling the accusations of the accuser (Revelation 12:10). The word "hypocrite" literally kept flashing in my mind's eye over and over again. I could almost hear Satan's hiss of "hypocrite." All weekend long, Satan was whispering in my ear, "If those people really knew you, they wouldn't listen to you, and they wouldn't love you."

As the accuser, that's how he comes against us. He wants us to walk in guilt instead of walking in God's grace. He wears you down with a barrage of lies until finally he wears you out. In this case, I hadn't thrown up my shield. I was convinced I was a counterfeit. A hypocrite. I had lowered my shield, and I was about to drop my sword. How could I preach?

I was standing on the wrong ground. Again, four times Paul says, *"Stand"*—stand on the finished work of the Son of God and the facts of the Word of God. Instead, I started standing on my work, and suddenly I didn't feel like I could qualify myself at all.

Here's the point: I haven't qualified myself to preach and be the pastor of my church. God has qualified me through the blood of the Lamb. I'm only qualified on any given day, no matter how well I'm living for God, by the blood of the Lamb.

I had brought down my shield, and I was standing on the wrong ground. I quit standing on Christ's ground, and I quit standing on Calvary's ground. I started standing on my ground. I came into the church office on Monday morning and I was undone. I was having an Isaiah 6:5 moment. Isaiah was a prophet with a potty mouth, and when he got in the presence of God, he said, *"Woe is me, for I am undone! Because I am a man of unclean lips, and I dwell in the midst of a people of unclean lips...."*

I was undone. I didn't feel like I could go on because whatever you think about me, I cannot stand in front of my church and say what I say if I'm not living it. I can't do it. I won't do it. On Monday morning, I told our staff that I didn't think I could do it. I didn't know what we were going to do, but I was going to call off revival week.

In that moment, my staff gathered around me, and they all laid hands on me and prayed for me. I was delivered that day, instantly! No more guilt. Monday night, I preached with more liberty, perhaps than I have ever preached before. In Second Corinthians 3:17 it says, *"Where the Spirit of the Lord is, there is liberty."* The Spirit of God spread throughout the auditorium that night and set many people free. Even after the service was over, people wouldn't leave. They continued to stay and sing because they were free! Truthfully, there might have even been some spontaneous dancing in that auditorium that night. That's what happens when a bunch of people get free in Christ.

I share that incident to teach you that you should never fight alone. I had fought alone. Satan had convinced me of another lie—that as the "man of God," I couldn't be honest about my frailties. One of his tactics is isolation. He wants you to live in secrecy instead of true biblical community because he knows you weren't meant to fight solo. Only when I became honest with others and let them fight this battle with me, was I delivered from the assault of the enemy.

CHAPTER 14

THE POWER OF COMMUNITY: UNITING SHIELDS OF FAITH

And they continued steadfastly in the apostles' doctrine and fellowship, in the breaking of bread, and in prayers. Then fear came upon every soul, and many wonders and signs were done through the apostles. Now all who believed were together, and had all things in common, and sold their possessions and goods, and divided them among all, as anyone had need. So continuing daily with one accord in the temple, and breaking bread from house to house, they ate their food with gladness and simplicity of heart, praising God and having favor with all the people. And the Lord added to the church daily those who were being saved (Acts 2:42-47).

The shield of a Roman soldier was designed to work with the shields of other soldiers, moving in formation. Unlike other ancient warriors of the same era, most of whom used round shields, a Roman soldier's shield was rectangular—for a very important reason. A Roman soldier was taught never to fight alone. His shield was meant to be used with the shields of others to make one gigantic shield.

Paul calls our shield the *"shield of faith."* There is supernatural power in the multiplied faith of the body and those with whom you're in community. When we move and march in unity as one body, we put our faith shields together and form an impregnable shield around each of us individually as well as corporately. What a picture God is giving us of the importance of unity!

A Roman soldier was taught to move as a unit. He was going to march and move and fight in formation. His rectangular shield, along with others in his unit, became a fortress around the entire unit of men. One of the formations every Roman soldier would have been taught early in his training was the Turtle Formation. This is how they marched into battle with their shields together, protecting them from the bombardment of arrows from the enemy. They would all be fully protected from the front as the ones in front put their shields side by side. Then the ones in the middle of the formation raised their shields above their heads. The ones on the sides of the formation put their shields together protecting their flanks.

By working together, every man in that formation was fully protected on all sides from the falling, flaming arrows of the enemy. Only as every soldier chose to march with others and move with others and stay in formation with others, could they be fully protected. If even one soldier broke out of formation, the entire army would suffer.

Through the shield of faith, God is teaching us that as the body of Christ, we are much stronger together than we could ever be apart. There is power in the multiplied faith of others. When we put our shields of faith together and we stand together, our collective faith becomes a fortress that Satan cannot penetrate. However, our multiplied faith together only works when we march in formation, in unity, as one body against the enemy.

Satan wants you to live in secrecy because the strength of sin is in its secrecy.

Only when you choose to march with others and fight with others and stay in formation are you fully protected. This is the power of James 5:16, *"Confess your trespasses one to another, and pray for one another, that you may be healed...."* Satan wants you to live in secrecy because the strength of sin is in its secrecy. You are a prisoner of war living in isolation. But when you choose to seek community in the body of Christ with authenticity and transparency, the strength of the enemy is broken.

I want this to burn into your mind's eye because this is how God intends for you to live as a Christian. A Roman soldier could not protect all of his sides marching solo. Only as he stayed in formation was he protected from the front, side, rear, and even overhead because he was putting his shield with others.

That's precisely how God intends for us to march forward as a unified army waging war as the body of Christ. No army on earth could have any hope of defeating their enemy if their only battle strategy was to tell all their troops to go fight the enemy however they wanted, whenever they wanted, and with whomever they wanted. "It doesn't matter, just go find somebody to fight." Now there's no coordination and no cooperation. It is nothing but chaos on the battlefield with every individual troop and every individual soldier running around fighting their own enemy in their own little skirmish.

MOVING TOGETHER

The average church in the United States makes no attempt to strategically coordinate their movements against the adversary. We are stronger when we stand together and move together than we could ever be individually. We must move together strategically in a coordinated movement against the adversary. This is how enemies and armies wage war.

Only as an army coordinates the movement of thousands and thousands of troops can they have any hope of success. Every local church around the world is representative of the body of Christ. Just like a formation of the Roman soldiers, the success of every local church lies in its ability to operate with careful, strategic, coordinated movements. Only then can we advance against our enemy.

It's no different from a football team. Imagine what would happen if the coach called the play into the huddle, and then all eleven men in the huddle decide they don't like the play. One player says, "I'm going to run this play," and another says, "Well, you can run that play, but I'm running this play." Another chimes in and says, "I don't like that play, I'm running this play." Another says, "I don't like any of those plays, I'm running this play." So the ball is snapped, and there are eleven "so-called" team members all running a different play. For a team to be successful, all eleven men have to be running the same play at the same time. That's true of anything in life.

Corporate America gets it, the sports world gets it, the military world gets it, but church people somehow don't always get it. It takes a united effort to advance against the adversary. Only then can we have any hope of being the Church that God intended, the Church that takes ground from the enemy.

Here's the point: Nobody can do it alone. If we truly want victory over the forces of darkness, we must be unified in our efforts to defeat the adversary, so we are all running the same play at the same time.

Heaven only knows what we can do for God's glory against the enemy when we are united in our faith and our purpose. A church is more than a fellowship—it's a WAR-ship meant to wage war for the souls of people, advance against the enemy, and take new territory for God's glory.

If I'm going to war, I want the biggest army I can possibly muster. Being large as an army is not necessarily a threat unless we are strategically united in a coordinated movement against our enemy. This is one of the fundamental strategies of battle I learned as a member of a SWAT team of seven highly-trained police officers to battle against people who were armed and dangerous.

Our survival was completely dependent on moving together as though we were one. You cannot think independently; you have to think as a unit. You cannot move independently; you have to move strategically as one unit against your adversary. This is exactly what God intended for His army to do in our day-to-day battles against the forces of darkness in our world.

Every person on a SWAT team has a specific assignment; no two officers are ever watching the same door or looking in the same direction at the same time. All sides are covered, and someone is always watching your back while you're watching someone else's back. God intends us to be like a Roman army or a SWAT team of sorts—to go against our adversary by coordinating our movements and making a strategic advance.

Jesus was speaking prophetically in Matthew 16:18 when He says, *"On this rock I will build My church, and the gates of Hades shall not prevail against it."* When we become that kind of church, we're unstoppable for God's glory and we're a threat to the enemy.

UNITED WE STAND

Wherever God is moving, Satan is marching and opposing. He knows he cannot stop us when we march together and move together. It's an old military strategy that has been around since the dawn of warfare to divide and conquer your enemy. If your enemy is too strong, divide them, fragment them, and fracture their ranks. Satan's strategy has always been to divide and conquer the enemy which is the Church of Jesus Christ. That is why it has suffered so many fractures, splinters, splits, and divisions through the years. This is always the strategy of an inferior adversary when fighting a superior army.

Consider the Battle of Teutoburg Forest, for example. It's also an example of one of the rarest things to happen in all of world history—a Roman loss on the battlefield. It was a devastating defeat and utter annihilation of three Roman legions plus their cohorts and auxiliaries. As many as twenty thousand Roman soldiers were massacred. It was the year AD 9 and Rome was attempting to expand their empire into what is today Germany. The Germanic tribes knew individually they were no match for Rome so they united. Getting people to work together was as rare in the ancient world as it is in our modern world!

The Germanic tribes were united behind Arminius, a German who had been trained as an officer in the Roman army, having received Roman citizenship. He defected when commanded to lay siege to his homeland, the place of his birth. Since he was a trained officer in the Roman army, he knew exactly how to defeat them.

He lured the Roman Legions into the Teutoburg Forest, where they would have to march single file instead of marching in formation. The Roman legions were now spread out single file for a distance of over ten miles. The Germans waited in the dense forest to ambush the Romans, who would never see them coming until it was too late. They began by attacking their center, dividing them down the middle in several places, completely fragmenting the legions. Since the Romans couldn't fight in formation, they were left to fight alone in single hand-to-hand skirmishes. It was a massacre. The Romans were decimated. It's believed that not a single Roman soldier made it out of the forest. After that humiliating massacre, Rome never again attempted to expand its empire east of the Rhine River.

That is exactly how Satan wars against us. He knows he is overmatched when we stand together, so he tries to get us to stand alone. In some parts of the world, Satan's primary tactic is persecution. In the United States, his primary tactic is not persecution but rather infiltration, inner corruption, erosion, and division.

Just as America's enemies abroad know we are much too strong militarily to be conquered from without, they have sent terrorist cells to infiltrate from within—individuals who work among us and live among us. They look like one of us and sometimes act like one of us, but they are not one of us. They are secretly, covertly working with our enemies to destroy us—not from the outside but from the inside.

The Church cannot be destroyed from the outside. Historically, wherever the Church has been persecuted, whether it was the early Roman persecutions, behind the Iron Curtain of twentieth century European communism, or today throughout the Islamic world or communist China, the Church only grows stronger. The Church in the U.S., however, is growing weaker—not because of attacks from the outside, but attacks from the inside.

What Satan cannot accomplish from the outside, he accomplishes from the inside. Just like Islamic terrorists who wage war against our nation, Satan wages war against the Church. He sends in his emissaries—satanic terrorists who covertly and secretly cause havoc from within—to blow things up from within, to cause division and discord, to weaken our defenses, and ultimately to divide us so he can conquer us. He knows that as long as we stand together and move in unity to advance strategically against the enemy, he cannot stop us.

SHEPHERDS, SHEEP, WOLVES

Jesus taught there are three kinds of people: shepherds, sheep, and wolves in sheep's clothing. Jesus said the wolves in sheep's clothing outwardly look like sheep, but inwardly they are ravenous wolves who come to steal, kill, and destroy (John 10:10).

How can we possibly discern such diabolical deception? Jesus says in Matthew 7:16, *"You will know them by their fruits."* You can begin to sense when someone might be a wolf in sheep's clothing when their pride begins to surface. Pride in your life makes you susceptible to the enemy, easily manipulated by the enemy, and a puppet for the enemy. Pride is one of the flaming arrows most used by the adversary. Pride was the fuel of Lucifer's rebellion when he was the anointed cherub, no longer satisfied sitting in the second chair. Pride is still the fuel of all kinds of rebellion, division, infighting, and backbiting.

Many times people are unwitting victims of Satan. They have no idea they are working for the enemy. You know what's inside them when they don't get their way or they don't get what they want. Sooner or later, whatever is inside is going to come out. That's why we are all called to be more than mere sheep. We are all called to be sheep dogs. A good guard dog is fiercely loyal, loving, and gentle to the people he is supposed to protect. But when he senses a threat to the family he is protecting, he will quickly go into attack mode. He will bark loud and bite hard.

We need a combat mentality when it comes to guarding our church's unity. That's how I live, and if you love your church, you should too.

PART VII

WINNING THE WAR WITHIN

THE HELMET OF SALVATION

Finally, my brethren, be strong in the Lord and in the power of His might. Put on the whole armor of God, that you may be able to stand against the wiles of the devil. For we do not wrestle against flesh and blood, but against principalities, against powers, against the rulers of the darkness of this age, against spiritual hosts of wickedness in the heavenly places. Therefore take up the whole armor of God, that you may be able to withstand in the evil day, and having done all, to stand. Stand therefore, having girded your waist with truth, having put on the breastplate of righteousness, and having shod your feet with the preparation of the gospel of peace; above all, taking the shield of faith with which you will be able to quench all the fiery darts of the wicked one. And take the helmet of salvation, and the sword of the Spirit, which is the word of God (Ephesians 6:10-17).

My good friend Bob Kuehl was gracious enough to endorse this book. Today he is Deputy Chief of Police for the KCPD, and he knows

183

all too well how the helmet is an essential piece of equipment when facing a dangerous adversary. As a young officer, long before I ever knew I would be a pastor and long before Bob could have imagined that he would rise through the ranks to hold the second-highest position in the entire department, Bob Kuehl was a young sergeant. Providentially, I was assigned to his supervision as a young officer while working the streets of Kansas City. I immediately connected with the young sergeant and grew to respect him for his character and compassion, tied to his humility and tenacity.

I grew to respect Bob even more after learning his story. Several years earlier, before I joined the police department and before he was promoted to sergeant, he was a young officer himself working the dangerous streets of KC. One night he responded to a disturbance call involving two brothers on PCP fighting with each other and their mother. He took one of the brothers into custody, and as he was escorting him away from the scene, the other brother picked up a piece of concrete the size of a soccer ball. Because of the PCP in his system, he threw it all the way across the yard and it struck Bob's head.

The injury was devastating and easily could have killed him. It probably would have killed him if he hadn't turned around right before the concrete hit him. If he had been struck in the back of the head, the injury would have been much more serious. At a minimum, he should have suffered irreversible brain damage. But after emergency brain surgery to remove several pieces of concrete from deep inside his head, by the grace of God he went on to make a full recovery.

The helmet is one of the most iconic pieces of armor in both modern and ancient warfare. As a member of the KCPD, a riot helmet was standard issue for every officer. It was essential to protect perhaps the most important part of your body from flying debris, rocks, bricks, and bottles in a riot situation.

Once I became a member of the KCPD Tactical Team, I was issued a second helmet. It was the same helmet worn by the modern U.S. military. It was made of Kevlar and was capable of protecting one's head from shrapnel and small arms ammunition.

When I first began studying the Bible, it seemed odd to me that Paul tells us to take up the helmet of salvation when as Christians we already have salvation. Fully understanding what it means to put on the helmet of salvation begins with an understanding that you are a three-part being—body, soul, and spirit—and that you must be saved on all three levels.

The apostle Paul wrote in Romans 10:13, that *"whoever calls on the name of the Lord shall be saved."* When you called on the name of Jesus, He forgave you of sin's penalty; He saved you from sin's penalty, but there's so much more you received in return.

JUSTIFICATION, SANCTIFICATION, GLORIFICATION

The first part of salvation is what Scripture calls *justification,* which is the salvation of your spirit. The moment you trusted Jesus Christ as your Lord and Savior, He forgave you of sin's penalty, and God declared you justified. As you read in an earlier chapter, in the eyes of God, it's as if you have never sinned. He cancels your sin account, and He no longer holds your sin against you. In the eyes of God, you are innocent of sin because of the Lamb of God who was slain for all our sin.

God forgives us of our sin and justifies us in His eyes.

At the moment of your salvation when you called upon Jesus and gave your life to Him, the Spirit of God came into your life and gave life to your spirit. Jesus said in John 3:3 that you must be *"born again"* because you came into this world physically alive but spiritually dead.

The second part of salvation is *sanctification*—the salvation of our soul. The soul is made up of the mind, the will, and the emotions. God wants to save us in terms of how we think and feel. He wants to save our mind, our will, and our emotions.

The moment you trusted in Jesus Christ as your Savior, your spirit was reborn, but your mind stayed the same. Your justification happened instantly—you were saved from sin's penalty, but your sanctification happens gradually—being saved from sin's power. It's the process Paul described in Romans 8:29 as being *"conformed to the image of His Son."*

Here's the point: God's plan and the goal of the Christian life is for you to grow and become more and more like *the* Son of God.

He sent *the* Son of God to become a human so that believers could become like the Son of God. As a son or daughter of God, He wants you to become like *the* Son of God, having been born again as a child of God. As you grow spiritually in the knowledge of the Word of God and in your relationship with the God of the Word, He conforms you more and more to the image of Jesus Christ. You become more and more like Him. Now we can begin to understand why Paul tells us to take up the helmet of salvation. Our spirit no longer needs saving, but our minds still do—every single day!

Paul tells us how to put on the helmet of salvation in Romans 12:2, *"Do not be conformed to this world, but be transformed by the renewing of your mind...."* Paul is saying not to be like the rest of the world going along with the prevailing standards, attitudes, and practices of the day. As Christians we may be *in* this sin-sick world, but we are not *of* it. The mind must be renewed daily.

Renew your mind daily.

God tells you to put on the helmet of salvation to help you guard your thoughts and emotions, giving your mind more and more to God's thoughts instead of sinful thoughts. It is called the helmet of salvation for a reason. It was a staple of the Roman infantry. A Roman helmet was for the purpose of protecting a soldier's head.

The Roman helmet is an iconic symbol of the ancient Roman Empire. While it could be very ornate depending on the rank of the soldier, it served a very practical purpose. A Roman soldier would not have dreamed of going into battle without protecting his head. If his head were to take a hit from an enemy blow of some kind, he could instantly be either knocked out of the battle or killed.

God has given you the helmet of salvation for the very same reason the Roman soldier needed his helmet. He wore it to protect his head from physical blows. As a soldier in God's army, we wear it to protect our mind, our thoughts, and our emotions from enemy blows, the enemy artillery, and the assault of the enemy. The helmet of salvation—daily renewing your mind in the Word of God—is to assist you in the process of sanctification by guarding your thoughts and your emotions.

Here's the point: The battle spiritually is always for the mind; Satan wants to control your mind. Whoever or whatever controls your mind controls you.

The third phase of salvation is glorification. Paul wrote in Romans 8:30, *"Moreover whom He predestined, these He also called; whom He called, these He also justified; and whom He justified, these He also **glorified**."* Glorification is the salvation of your body. Our bodies are under the curse of Adam's sin, destined to decay and return to dust. The older you get, the more you notice your body changing. When you get up in the morning, your joints are stiff, your eyesight begins to dim, and you start losing hair where you are supposed to have it, and you start growing hair where you are not supposed to have it. It's the curse of Adam's sin.

The good news is there's a day coming in heaven, the Bible says, when we are all going to get an upgrade. The Bible says we are going to get a new body—the resurrected body of the Lord Jesus Christ. It will be a body that will never get sick, never grow old, and never die. So you see all three phases of salvation—the salvation of the spirit, the salvation of the soul, and the salvation of the body. But in between our justification and our glorification is the sometimes long and difficult process of sanctification—the salvation of the mind, will, and emotions.

As we wait for that day of our glorification, the apostle Paul gives us a battle strategy to wage war for our mind by putting on the helmet of salvation daily. He began by writing to the Ephesian church, and now he's writing to the Corinthian church. Second Corinthians 10:3 says, *"For though we walk in the flesh, we do not war according to the flesh."* That is also what he writes in Ephesians 6:12, *"We do not wrestle against flesh and blood."*

Paul reminds us that although we live in the physical, we do not war after the physical. Though we walk in the flesh, our real warfare is not with anything that is of the flesh or of the physical world. In Second Corinthians 10:4, Paul says, *"For the weapons of our warfare are not carnal* [or physical] *but mighty in God for pulling down strongholds,"* meaning enemy strongholds and fortifications. Paul was pointing out to the Corinthians they had spiritual weapons because they were in spiritual warfare, just as we have weapons. We can win, and he gives us the battle strategy. This is how we put on our helmet of salvation.

CHAPTER 15

WHO'S IN CHARGE? GOD'S CHAIN OF COMMAND

Casting down arguments and every high thing that exalts itself against the knowledge of God, bringing every thought into captivity to the obedience of Christ (2 Corinthians 10:5).

Have you ever been in a situation where nobody knew who was in charge and everything was in chaos? When either everybody thought they were in charge or nobody did? As a parent, my kids better know I have the authority in our home.

WEAPONS OF OUR WARFARE

Anytime two armies are at war, there is always a chain of command. Remember, God does everything through a chain of command. God created you with a chain of command.

Here's the point: Apart from authority there is anarchy, and Satan would love nothing more than for you to live in a state of anarchy! You can only win this war as you follow the chain of command.

As a born-again child of God, you are a triune being. You now bear the image of God in that you are three in one. You have a spirit, soul, and body that represent God's chain of command in your life. God established it to bring every human being into alignment with Him to live victoriously and triumphantly against the enemy.

The chain of command begins with the Spirit, in conjunction with your spirit; they are now one with each other as a born-again child of God. The Spirit of God came to live inside of you the moment you received the Son of God (Romans 8:9). You are now permanently indwelt by God's Spirit (see Ephesians 1:13, 4:30). Underline this! *The Spirit in union with your spirit is meant to rule the soul, and the soul is meant to rule the body.* The body is meant to obey the soul, and the soul is meant to obey the spirit. That is what it means to be a "Spirit-filled" Christian or to live the "Spirit-filled" life. It's when you are submitting to the control of the Spirit of God in your life. You are indwelt by God's Spirit permanently, but you must be filled with God's Spirit repeatedly (Ephesians 5:18).

Notice how many times that chain of command is reversed and how many times we allow our bodies to give the orders and our bodies to call the shots. The body gives the command and the mind simply obeys and falls in line and says, "Okay," while the spirit stands by idly doing nothing.

Think about how many times the body says, "I need that nicotine," or "I need ice cream." The mind says, "Okay. Let me get that for you." Just last night I ate an entire bag of kettle corn. I don't mean a small individual bag. I mean one of the family-size bags.

The Bible says to confess your faults one to another (James 5:16). I am confessing that not twenty-four hours ago as I am writing this, I consumed an entire bag of kettle corn! It was pure gluttony. Normally I try to have a little discipline. I knew I shouldn't keep eating, but it was oh, so pleasing to the palate. Some people enjoy something salty, while others enjoy something sweet. But I am both sweet and salty, and kettle corn is one of my weaknesses. My body said, "Keep feeding me" and my mind said, "Okay!" And I completely ignored the spirit's prompting, "Come on, Phil. Put down the bag. You've had enough."

Anytime we seek to gratify our physical bodies apart from the will of God, we give in to the *"lust of the flesh"* (First John 2:16). Overeating kettle corn might make you feel sick for a few hours, but imagine if it's an addiction to cocaine, methamphetamine, pornography, or sexual immorality! Satan, like a thief, has stolen our victory and led us back into captivity, all because we failed to follow the chain of command. The body is not meant to *give* orders, it's meant to *take* orders.

When we let the gratification of our physical bodies rule our lives, we become fleshly Christians, and our actions will always lead to our destruction. A fleshly Christian is controlled by the flesh instead of being controlled by their spirit. Carnal or fleshly Christians allow the body to be in the driver's seat, while the mind obeys and the spirit stands idly by.

How many times do you wake up early on a Sunday morning to go to church? As believers, God commands us not to forsake *"the assembling of ourselves together"* (Hebrews 10:25). But it's overcast, and you can hear the gentle sound of falling rain. It's a perfect day to sleep in. Your body says, "I'm tired, roll over and go back to sleep." The mind "amens" the body, the spirit does nothing, and you are off to slumberland again. A carnal Christian is someone who allows the physical cravings of their flesh to be in control.

Soulish Christians are completely controlled by their emotions and feelings. The spirit is meant to rule the soul, not the other way around. Instead of being controlled by the spirit, so many Christians are controlled by their souls. Remember, your emotions are tied to your soul, which are your thoughts and emotions. Soulish Christians allow themselves to be completely feelings-driven, feelings-led, and at the mercy of their emotions. Their feelings are hurt, and they can't let it go. They are unable to forgive even though God commands us to forgive others.

They feel anger so they are prone to outbursts of wrath. They, and everyone else in their lives, are at the mercy of their anger issues. They feel bitterness over the hardships they face in life, even though God commands us to have joy. Eventually, they turn into grumpy old men and sour old women. They lack lasting victory because they are completely at the mercy of their emotions. Satan knows exactly which buttons to push to control them day in and day out, and he controls their emotions at will.

On the other hand, Spirit-filled Christians are followers of Jesus who have received the infilling of God's Holy Spirit. These believers walk and live in God's chain of command. When the spirit is in control as God intended, it is ruling the mind, the mind is ruling the body, and both the body and the mind are living in submission to the control of God's Spirit in their life.

You are in submission mentally, emotionally, and physically to the control of the Spirit of God in your life. "I am letting the Spirit of God control my thoughts and emotions, and then, in turn, my thoughts are controlling my actions." That's what it means to be a Spirit-filled follower.

This is the battle strategy Paul lays out for us in Second Corinthians 10:3-5. It's how you put on the helmet of salvation every day to protect yourself from the mental and emotional attacks from the enemy.

When you are being controlled by the Spirit and *"filled with the Spirit"* (Ephesians 5:18), it will lead to a life overflowing with the *"fruit of the Spirit."* Galatians 5:16 says, *"I say then: Walk in the Spirit, and you shall not fulfill the lust of the flesh."* Galatians 5:22-23 tells us, *"But the fruit of the Spirit is love, joy, peace, longsuffering, kindness, goodness, faithfulness, gentleness, self-control...."* The Spirit-filled life is full of love and joy and peace! It's the supernatural ability to suffer long—to be patient! It's the supernatural, God-given ability to show kindness to your enemies. It's the ability to have self-control (even with kettle corn) when otherwise you would be out of control.

You can see why Satan is relentlessly waging war on your soul. He wants to control your mind and emotions, and he wants to control your soul so it won't be ruled by God's Spirit. He wants to take you captive and hold you in slavery so you won't live in victory and experience what Jesus calls "life abundantly."

BATTLE FOR THE HIGH GROUND

> *Casting down arguments and every high thing that exalts itself against the knowledge of God...* (2 Corinthians 10:5).

Paul is writing about the high ground of your mind. Your mind will either be a stronghold of God or a stronghold of Satan. It will either be an elevated and fortified position for the Holy Spirit or one of Satan's spirits.

Wars have been won and lost over whichever army could take and hold the high ground because they will win that battle. You see it historically and militarily.

Your mind will either be a stronghold of God or a stronghold of Satan.

A great illustration is one of the most famous battles of World War II, the Battle of Iwo Jima. The Allied forces needed to take Iwo Jima. There was no way to win the war in the South Pacific without it. The island is only eleven square miles, but they needed it strategically in order to control the Japanese Air Force and the landing strip on Iwo Jima. The problem was the Japanese were fully fortified on Mount Suribachi, an elevated position from which the Japanese could defend the entire island from the Allied invasion. They had the advantage.

The Allied forces knew it was going to cost a great deal of blood and sacrifice, but they decided it was worth it. Our Marines went up that hill over and over and over again. It took them thirty-six days to finally take that mountain because the Japanese had the advantage, but it was the turning point in the battle. Although it took twenty-six thousand U.S. casualties, including seven thousand dead, they finally won the battle of Iwo Jima. Who can forget that iconic American image of our U.S. Marines going up one last time and hoisting the U.S. flag on Mount Suribachi? They literally won that high ground with their blood, which meant they could now take the entire island.

Here's the point: Whoever takes the high ground controls the entire island!

There was a day 2,000 years ago when Jesus Christ walked up the high ground of another mountain called Mount Calvary where He shed His blood and died in our place. Because you've been bought with a price, you have already gained the high ground through Jesus Christ. He has posted His flag over your life. Song of Solomon 2:4 says that His banner over you is love. He owns everything and has all power and authority over you. This also means Satan has no power or authority whatsoever over any area of your life.

Don't think for a moment that every day Satan doesn't come looking for an opportunity to take it back. The battle, however, is for the mind. He wants to take over your mind, thoughts, and emotions. Because Jesus has won the high ground, you simply have to stand your ground and defend it. And defending the high ground is a lot easier than trying to take it back once you've lost it. That is why Paul says four times in Ephesians 6, *"Stand"*—stand your ground.

CHAPTER 16

DON'T GIVE PLACE TO THE ENEMY

For though we walk in the flesh, we do not war according to the flesh. For the weapons of our warfare are not carnal but mighty in God for pulling down strongholds, casting down arguments and every high thing that exalts itself against the knowledge of God, bringing every thought into captivity to the obedience of Christ (2 Corinthians 10:3-5).

We have a fortified position, and our adversary cannot touch us, but that doesn't mean he's giving up on us. The word "stronghold" in this verse means "mountain fortress" in the Greek language. Paul was writing in terms that the Corinthians could easily identify. Every ancient city had an acropolis or an elevated, fortified position where they would flee during an enemy invasion. No doubt when they read that verse, their thoughts went immediately to their own fortress. The Corinthians understood the concept of a stronghold because they had a stronghold.

A few years ago, I stood in that very spot in the ruins of Corinth looking up at that mighty mountain fortress and stronghold of that ancient city. The Corinthians would have fled up this mountain where it was fortified. From this elevated, fortified position, they could defend their city from an attacking enemy. Satan is attacking your mind daily. Put on the helmet of salvation and get to that elevated and fortified position. Paul is teaching in Second Corinthians 10:3-5 that even if the adversary has built a stronghold in your mind, God has given you the weapons to break free and take it back! You have a stronghold already in Jesus Christ. From a military standpoint, you have the advantage.

Psalm 18:2-3 puts it this way:

> **The Lord is my rock** and my **fortress** and my **deliverer**; my God, my **strength**, in whom I will trust; my **shield** and the horn of my **salvation**, **my stronghold**. I will call upon the Lord, who is worthy to be praised; so shall I be saved from my enemies.

At the end of those two verses, the psalmist says, "*...so shall I be saved from my enemies.*" To put it in our terms today:

- So shall I be saved from this illicit, immoral relationship.

- So shall I be saved from pornography.

- So shall I be saved from emotional bondage.

- So shall I be saved from this addiction.

- So shall I be saved from discouragement, fear, depression, anxiety.

- So shall I be saved from all the fiery darts of the enemy.

The Lord Jesus Christ has posted His colors. But every single day Satan is warring against your mind because whoever holds the high ground controls the entire island.

Here's the point: You will either make your mind a mountain fortress for God, or it will become a mountain fortress for Satan.

The choice is yours. Your mind will either be a stronghold of Jesus and His power, or it will be a stronghold for all of the junk you have allowed to control you.

This is why Paul warns us in Romans 12:2, *"And do not be conformed to this world, but be transformed by the renewing of your mind."* The mind must be defended and guarded because Satan is always trying to take back ground that Jesus has won. It's a battle for your thoughts and a battle for your emotions, which is why Paul says in Second Corinthians 10:3, *"For though we walk in the flesh, we do not war according to the flesh."* Our real warfare is not physical; it's not anything you can see.

THE ENEMY'S FOCUS

If you are focused on something you can see, you are focused on the wrong front. That's exactly what the enemy wants you to do. He wants you to fight the war on the wrong front, so you don't fight the war on the right front. Practically, this means that the real fight and the real enemy is not with alcohol if you are an alcoholic, it's not with drugs if you are a drug addict, it's not with cigarettes if you are trying to kick the nicotine habit, it's not the food in the refrigerator if you are trying to eat less, and it's not the pornography on the computer, if pornography is your area of captivity.

Those are not the real enemies—they are simply the symptoms, not the source of the problem. They are simply the tools the enemy uses against you to wage war for your mind, your thoughts, and your emotions. They are the tools he uses to enslave you so you won't live in the freedom and liberty and victory that Jesus has already given you.

Sin does not begin out in the world; sin begins within our minds. You try to suppress your sin by doing better and trying harder. Victory is not through suppression, it's through submission as you submit yourself to the God-given chain of command. You find victory instead of defeat when you submit your mind to obey the spirit, then your body to obey your mind. Every day the devil will try to get you to take off your helmet of salvation and invert that chain of command. Satan cannot take that high ground from you unless he can entice you from your place of safety under the blood of Christ.

> Spiritual warfare is about winning the war within.

Spiritual warfare is about winning the war within. There is a struggle going on inside of us daily in some capacity. You cannot win anything outside unless you win the war inside. You must learn to reprogram your thought patterns that have been programmed over the course of your life by the world, the flesh, and the devil.

Satan does not have to destroy your body; it's already destined to be destroyed. He cannot destroy your spirit for it has been sealed by God's Spirit (Ephesians 4:30), so he targets your soul. Sin and Satan are at war with the Spirit of God for control of your soul or heart—your mind, your thoughts, and emotions.

In Second Corinthians 10:5, Paul gives us the key to victory: *"Casting down arguments and every high thing that exalts itself against the knowledge of God, bringing every thought into captivity to the obedience of Christ."*

The devil cannot take the high ground forcefully from you, but he is attempting to lure you down from it. He wants you to come down so that he can go up. He wants the ground that belongs to Jesus; he wants the ground that belongs to God. He wants you to come down and willfully abandon the high ground so he can take it.

Don't give place to the devil. Stand on the high ground!

God has set you on the high ground, but it is up to you to defend it. This is what Paul meant when he warned us in Ephesians 4:27 not to *"give place to the devil"*—not to give the devil a foothold. That one short verse says so much. As a child of God, the devil has lost all place in your life. He can only have the power and authority you give back to him and the high ground you relinquish that was bought with the blood of Jesus Christ.

Don't be lured down through thoughts or emotions or through some tribulation or temptation. Don't give place to the devil over your thoughts or emotions or any area in your life, and *"make no provision for the flesh, to fulfill its lusts"* (Romans 13:14). In other words, don't think about how to gratify the desires of the flesh. Stand firm on the high ground of Jesus Christ, and don't listen to Satan's lies. Don't give the devil any room within your mind. When you watch ungodly television programs, ungodly movies, read ungodly magazines, or listen to ungodly music with all of its sin and sickness and sensuality and permissiveness and pornography, you are being lured down from the high ground.

> Your mind is either going to be a stronghold of Satan or a stronghold of God.

Militarily, if you are already elevated and you are fortified, you have a great advantage to defend your position. That is why Paul urges us all to stay on the high ground and not let Satan lure you down. In John 8:44, Jesus says of the devil, *"...When he speaks a lie, he speaks from his own resources, for he is a liar and the father of it."* When Satan speaks, he speaks a lie because *"there is no truth in him."* Sometimes his lies are very subtle, and he will cloak the truth with a little bit of a lie. It's still a lie, but it looks like the truth. Satan cannot tell the truth. He has to lie because that is all he has.

My father is a veteran of the U.S. Army, serving from 1963-1965 in the 25th Infantry Division. He specialized in mortars, light artillery. He was trained to make mathematical calculations based on the distance to the front lines of the enemy. Those calculations would enable my father to set the exact trajectory of the mortar to land precisely in the front lines and fortified positions of the enemy. Before the front-line advances on the enemy's front line, the strategy of any battle is to have already blown holes in the enemy's fortifications with mortars and other artillery.

Satan does the same thing every time he lobs his lies, like enemy artillery, into strategic areas of vulnerability in your life. His lies are the mortars he uses in an attempt to tear down your mental defenses and fortifications of God's Word over your mind.

NEVER DOUBT GOD'S LOVE

He weakens your walls of absolute truth by getting you to doubt the Word of God and the character of God. He wants to get you to doubt what God has said or who God is. When you begin to doubt the Word of God or the goodness of God, those defenses are weakened. Satan is luring you down off the high ground, and he's trying to advance his way up to the high ground of control over you. If something really bad happened to you, you might have thought to yourself, *If God really loved me, He wouldn't have allowed this to happen.* Satan just lobbed a lie into your mind, and suddenly you are doubting the character of God and doubting God's goodness.

Remember that is exactly what he did to Eve. In Genesis 3, *he didn't just attack the Word of God, he attacked the character of God.* "Eve, if God really loved you, why would He keep this from you? He's trying to hide something from you. He knows it's good, and He doesn't want you to have it. Eve, if God really loved you, He'd let you eat of this tree."

The moment the devil can get you to doubt what God has said or to doubt God's character, your fortifications begin to crack, and you are on your way down to Satan's control in your life. Once the fortifications guarding your mind come down, he has set the bait.

First come the lies, evil thoughts, and fantasies. Paul says in Second Corinthians 10:5 that we defend our position by *casting down arguments.* When he comes and argues against God, Satan puts a thought in your head that is contrary to the Word of God. It's an argument against the Word of God that graphically illustrates what Satan is trying to do in your mind.

Pornography is so destructive against the human soul because those mental images are forever locked in your mind. You can never be rid of them. They remain there for Satan to pull out and use against you anytime he wants. That's why Proverbs 4:23 says, *"Keep your heart with all diligence, for out of it spring the issues of life."*

God has given you the breastplate of righteousness to guard your heart and the helmet of salvation to guard your mind. The heart has to do with attitudes and emotions; our mind has to do with our thoughts and meditations. It's critical that we guard both our heart and mind because Satan will introduce a sinful thought or fantasy into them that will gradually lure you down the hill and into captivity.

GUARD YOUR HEART AND MIND

When Satan introduces an ungodly thought, an ungodly fantasy, or an ungodly emotion, instead of casting it out immediately like Paul says in Second Corinthians 10:5, you let it linger. The longer it lingers, the more you begin to enjoy it. After days, weeks, or even months, you begin to really entertain it, and now you are meditating on it. Eventually, Satan knows you will enact it. His deceptive path goes from enjoying, to entertaining, to enacting. It might take days, weeks, months, or years. Our carnal minds are just that corrupt. He doesn't care how long it takes as long as he can lure you down so he can take the high ground, a strategic position from which he can destroy you.

Most people don't wake up in the morning thinking, *"Today would be a good day to commit the sin of adultery. Maybe I'll try that sin today. I think today I'm going to blow up my ministry, or I'm going to blow up my family, or I'm going to blow up my marriage."* That's not how it happens.

He not only wants to control you through lies, deception, and ungodly thoughts, but also through your emotions. He wants to control you through negative feelings and negative emotions.

Emotions are one of the greatest strongholds Satan has in his arsenal—discouragement, dejection, depression, anger, bitterness, unforgiveness. Discouraged, defeated Christians are no threat to the enemy. They are POWs, prisoners of war. Many Christians, unfortunately, are prisoners of their emotions. They're in bondage to bitterness or unforgiveness.

CHAPTER 17

HOLDING THE HIGH GROUND

For though we walk in the flesh, we do not war according to the flesh. For the weapons of our warfare are not carnal but mighty in God for pulling down strongholds, casting down arguments and every high thing that exalts itself against the knowledge of God, bringing every thought into captivity to the obedience of Christ (2 Corinthians 10:3-5).

How do we counter Satan's assault? How do we stay behind our fortification? How do we put on our helmet of salvation? Paul gives us the answer: *"casting down arguments and every high thing that exalts itself against the knowledge of God."* The high things that Paul is alluding to in Second Corinthians

10:5 are idols we have built up in our minds. High places in the Old Testament were places of idol worship. Pagans in ancient days would find the highest hill or the highest place to erect their pagan altars and Ashtoreth poles. Over time, they became known as the high places.

God sits in a high and holy place. It should come as no surprise that Satan wants the high place. In the days of King Solomon, the people of God stopped tearing down the high places and the idols. They didn't worship them, but they stopped tearing them down. Because they failed to tear down the idols, the next generation began worshiping the idols and fell into idolatry. Within just a few more generations, because of their idolatry, they were led into captivity.

Just as surely, Satan wants to lead you out of that place of victory and life abundantly where you are walking in the liberty of Jesus Christ. He wants you to go back to the slavery of sin and the captivity of Satan. It always begins with idolatry.

In verse 5, Paul is writing specifically of the idolatry in our mind—those mental idols that we have allowed to linger, that we have entertained, toyed with, or worshiped. He's saying we are to tear down the high things mentally that exalt themselves against the knowledge of God because just like the idolatry of Israel led them into captivity, our idolatry will also lead us into captivity. Paul is urging us to tear down the idolatry in our lives—the unclean thoughts and emotions that you have allowed to linger in your mind so long they have taken up residence.

You can't just tear those idols down. You must replace them, or Satan will come back with something even stronger. Tear down that ungodly altar and then build a godly altar in your mind. Make your mind a stronghold of God instead of a stronghold of Satan. Replace that ungodly mental image or thought with a godly mental image or thought. If Satan hisses in your ear, "God doesn't love you," you must immediately erect a godly altar from God's absolute truth found in John 3:16: *"For God so loved the world that He gave His only begotten Son..."* and declare: Yes, God does love me!

Perhaps Satan hisses, "You are a hypocrite, and you are not worthy. Who are you to say that you are a Christian?" When he wants you to walk in guilt instead of grace for sins that have long since been forgiven, you immediately erect a godly altar. Remember, First John 2:1 says, *"We have an Advocate with the Father, Jesus Christ the righteous."*

Your faith declaration: I have been set free. I'm a child of God. I'm an heir of the King. I am ransomed and redeemed. I am innocent of sin. I am not walking in guilt. I'm walking in grace, and I'm not coming down from the high ground Jesus won for me. I'm standing firmly on God's Word.

Satan lobs in another mortar, "You have no hope for your marriage, your marriage is too far gone, there's no hope. You might as well just give up, give in, and get a divorce." You immediately erect a godly altar. In Ephesians 3:20, God says He is *able to do exceedingly abundantly above all that we ask or think, according to the power that works in us."*

Your faith declaration: Satan, you are a liar! Jesus is the truth-teller. Jesus said in Matthew 19:26, *"With men this is impossible, but with God all things are possible."* "There *is* hope for my marriage. I'm not giving up, I'm not giving in, and I'm not coming down. This is God's ground, and I'm standing firm in my position!"

Now name the ungodly thought, the ungodly emotion, the idolatry, and bring *"every thought into captivity to the obedience of Christ."* The moment you realize you have a thought that is disobedient to God's Word, you immediately have to cast it down, take the thought captive, and replace your thought with a God thought.

The longer you let the ungodly thought linger, the farther downhill you are being lured. Remember, it's harder to take that ground back once you've given it up. The best thing you can do is to follow Paul's instruction. Put on the helmet of salvation every day, taking every thought captive.

There is no rest in warfare.

You may be thinking, *Well, Phil, I might have to do this twenty-five times a day.* No, you might have to do it twenty-five times in a *minute*. I know, I've been there! It is never one and done. It's the hard work of warfare. There is no rest in warfare.

BULLDOG-LIKE FAITH

You win the battle for the mind by being diligent in guarding your mind and casting down every thought that is not of God. You don't have to take the high ground, but you must defend it with your faith confession. When you do, that thought will not stay, that thought will not stick. You're casting it out and tearing it down. You erect a God thought and refuse to let go of it with bulldog-like faith in the power of God's Word. Whether you're defending the high ground or trying to take back the high ground, you do it exactly the same way.

Maybe emotions are your problem and where you are vulnerable to Satan's attacks. You cannot always help how you feel, but you can always help what you think. Some Christians are emotional basket cases. If that's you, please know I'm not trying to be mean or speak down to you. I care about you, and I've written this book to help you. Someone who will read this book may be completely at the mercy of his or her emotions. Satan may have even held you in bondage for years, and you never realized it until now. For some people, it's their thoughts; for others, it's their emotions. Your emotions and thoughts are intertwined.

Here's the point: Right thoughts eventually produce right feelings.

God never commands us to change how we feel because we can't. God created us with godly feelings of compassion, love, and joy, as well as sorrow, remorse, and yes, even anger. Satan attempts to corrupt every one of those feelings and use them against you. Some people say they can't help it when they are sexually attracted to the same gender or to the attractive girl or guy in the office when they have a loving spouse at home. The key is whether you choose to embrace those feelings or reject them.

God wants us to learn to change how we think and respond to life's ups and downs. Paul doesn't say to bring captive every emotion. He doesn't say to bring captive every feeling. He says to bring captive every "thought," because right thinking will eventually produce right feelings. It won't happen immediately, but if you keep thinking what is right, you will eventually feel what is right. When you're feeling what is wrong, start thinking what is right.

GOD COMMANDS MOTION

Here's an example. You might feel sorrowful. It's a tough world where bad things happen. It has been cursed by sin, and because of sin, we live in a world of suffering. Perhaps you have suffered greatly and lost someone you love or you have gone through some other trial or tribulation. Maybe you've lost your job, and you are sorrowful. Who wouldn't feel sorrowful?

The Bible commands you to be joyful. God never commands an emotion, He commands motion.

Even though you feel sorrowful, if you have thoughts that are joyful and you focus your thoughts on things that are joyful and start considering all the things God has given you that are joyful, eventually you will stop feeling as sorrowful. If all you think about are the sorrowful things in your life, you have no hope of being anything but sorrowful.

You may have been held in bondage for years by bitterness and unforgiveness. Somebody betrayed you and hurt you. It might have been a spouse, friend, family member, or parent. Bitterness is bondage for you and you alone. After all you've been through and everything you've had to put up with—lies, betrayal—who wouldn't be bitter? You were wronged! Nevertheless, Jesus commands you in Ephesians 4:32 to *"be kind to one another...forgiving one another, even as God in Christ forgave you."*

You may not feel like forgiving, but God is not commanding an emotion—He's commanding a motion. You can choose as an act of your will to forgive and not hold a grudge. You can let their sin go because God has let your sin go—you can do for them what God did for you. Even though you don't feel it right away, if you start thinking it, you will eventually feel it. It might take weeks, months, or years, but eventually you'll be free.

You never want to follow your emotions or feelings because they can lead to captivity. What do you do when you feel attracted to someone you're not married to? Must you follow your feelings? I hope not. It will lead to your destruction just like Satan has led so many to their ruin. You must say, "No, I'm not following my feelings. I'm going to make God's thoughts, my thoughts." Adultery is depravity. It's ugly. It may have intensity, but it's not true intimacy.

Declare: Satan, you are a liar. However long it takes, I'm not going to give up, and I'm not going to give in. I'm going to hang on to this thought because I know eventually my feelings will follow. *I choose to follow God, and His power will overcome your lies.*

When you feel what is wrong, start thinking what is right. Eventually, the emotions will follow. Take hold of your thoughts and your mind.

Here's the point: If you do not take your thoughts captive, your thoughts will eventually take you captive, and that is right where the enemy wants you.

In our fight with the enemy, we must hold the high ground of our mind and emotions at all cost. However, there comes a time in all military campaigns when an army must stop defending and start advancing. In the days of close-quarters combat with rifles or muskets, that decision was announced with the order to "Fix bayonets!" For the Roman soldier it was, "Draw your swords!" That leads us to the next chapter. For the Kingdom warrior, there comes a point where it's time to "Draw your sword!"

PART VIII

UNLEASHING DIVINE POWER

THE SWORD OF THE SPIRIT

Finally, my brethren, be strong in the Lord and in the power of His might. Put on the whole armor of God, that you may be able to stand against the wiles of the devil. For we do not wrestle against flesh and blood, but against principalities, against powers, against the rulers of the darkness of this age, against spiritual hosts of wickedness in the heavenly places. Therefore take up the whole armor of God, that you may be able to withstand in the evil day, and having done all, to stand. Stand therefore, having girded your waist with truth, having put on the breastplate of righteousness, and having shod your feet with the preparation of the gospel of peace; above all, taking the shield of faith with which you will be able to quench all the fiery darts of the wicked one. And take the helmet of salvation, and the sword of the Spirit, which is the word of God (Ephesians 6:10-17).

We've made several observations in this study of the whole armor of God and its parallels between physical warfare and spiritual warfare.

God's armor brings victory because it is far more than a protective covering. It is the very life of Jesus Christ Himself. *"Put on the armor,"* wrote Paul in his letter to the Romans, *"Put on the Lord Jesus Christ"* (Romans 13:12-14).

It is my prayer that by now you have the key to victory firmly in your spirit—stand! Stand firmly on God's Word and defend your fortified position in Christ. Jesus bled and died in our place, and three days later He rose from the dead. His victory is our victory! Never forget that.

Even though Satan does not have authority over you, he is relentlessly attempting to gain back authority over you. He assaults your mind and your emotions, and he wants to control your thoughts. He wants to control your feelings because whether in ancient times or modern warfare, the importance of maintaining a high position is fundamental in military strategy. That's why we must hold the high ground.

HOLD THE FLANK!

"Hold the flank at all hazard!" was the command received by Lieutenant Colonel Joshua Chamberlain as he was commanding the 20th Maine Volunteer Infantry on perhaps the most important day of the American Civil War. The Civil War might have been won by the South had they been able to get to the high ground at the Battle of Gettysburg on July 2, 1863. General Robert E. Lee had taken the fight to the North. He had assaulted Union territory, leading his southern troops into the little town of Gettysburg in Pennsylvania.

The North was much better equipped, but the South was highly motivated, and they were led by some of the greatest military minds of the day. The South saw an opportunity to seize the high ground at the Battle of Gettysburg on the extreme left flank of the Union

Army on a hill called Little Round Top. If they could have taken this hill, they could have established a line that would have devastated the entire Union Army.

History tells us that a Union general by the name of G.K. Warren saw what was going on. He didn't check with superiors but immediately seized the moment. He commanded his Lieutenant Colonel Joshua Chamberlain to "Hold the flank at all hazard!" Chamberlain knew that if they gave up the high ground on Little Round Top, in all probability the Confederates would win the battle and perhaps even win the war. From the high ground, having flanked the Union Army, they would be able to subject the North to devastating losses. There would be nothing stopping them from marching clear into Washington, DC, just a three- or four-day's march away.

Chamberlain and his three hundred and fifty-eight men withstood wave after wave of Confederate troops from Alabama as they marched up the hill over and over again trying to take the high ground.

I personally had the privilege of standing on Little Round Top just a few years ago where this historic battle took place. I could feel a surge of adrenaline rushing through my body as I stood behind the huge boulders and other manmade fortifications of the 20th Maine. I could almost hear the cries of the wounded and dying. I could practically see the haze of gun smoke and feel the panic and pandemonium that must have filled the air on that hot July day in 1863.

The battle for Little Round Top went on for a full one and a half hours. With ammunition almost gone and many of his men dead or wounded, Chamberlain realized they could not continue to defend the high ground on the defensive. He made a risky, gutsy move, telling his men to "Fix bayonets." He was going to do something unconventional and almost unprecedented in military history. To defend the high ground, they were going to leave the safety of their elevated and fortified position. Moving as one single unit, the men of the 20th Maine charged down the hill into the face of their enemy.

As they saw the Confederates forming up at the bottom of the hill for yet another push uphill, Chamberlain gave the charge, and his entire unit came charging down the hill. They took their enemy completely by surprise, sweeping the Confederates off the hill once and for all! In the end, Chamberlain had held the high ground, and that single moment was probably the turning point in the war. The Union would go on to win the Battle of Gettysburg, and the South would never again threaten the North.

FROM DEFENSIVE TO OFFENSIVE

There is a lesson here to be learned for all of us as Kingdom warriors. At some point, you have to leave the defensive and go on the offensive. Chamberlain knew his men would have the advantage from the momentum of moving down the hill. He also knew his enemy wouldn't be expecting it and wouldn't be ready. It may have been the most famous infantry charge in American military history. It was an extremely risky move to leave their defensive position, but winning always demands risk. For the Kingdom warrior it's called faith.

Most of the armor of God recorded in Ephesians 6 is for defensive purposes. In fact, all of the armor that we studied so far is to equip you to defend the high ground. But eventually, in any conflict, you have to go on the offensive. There comes a point when you cannot remain on the defensive and win. That is why God has given us an offensive weapon—*"the sword of the Spirit, which is the word of God."* He wants us to use it to charge into the face of the adversary and take ground from the enemy.

Unlike the other pieces of the Roman armor that were meant to protect the soldier from injury inflicted by the enemy, the sword was meant to inflict injury *on* the enemy!

Our weapon is symbolically called the *"sword of the Spirit,"* which Paul immediately defines as *"the word of God."* Just as the Roman soldier had a weapon, we have a weapon as well. We need to learn what it is about a sword that is similar to the Word of God, a weapon in our hands.

First of all, we see that same symbolism in Hebrews 4:12, *"For the word of God is living and powerful, and sharper than any two-edged sword...."* A Roman soldier's sword was two-edged, unlike a sword in many cases with just one cutting edge.

Not only that, it's not the long sword that you see throughout medieval history that knights needed both hands to wield. You couldn't use a long sword with a shield. The Roman soldier went into battle with a shield in one hand and his sword in the other. The long sword was waved in battle with two hands into a mass of humanity, as it was swung over and over again to lop off heads and arms and anything else without much precision.

Whereas the Roman soldier's short sword was only about eighteen inches in length because it was meant for close, hand-to-hand combat. They stood in a skirmish line with a shield in one hand and a short sword in the other making precision strikes against the adversary. That should come as no surprise because God is teaching us to use His Word, the sword of the Spirit, with precision accuracy and precision strikes as well.

Most of the time in the New Testament, "word," as in the Word of God, is the Greek word *logos*. *Logos* is the entire *written* revelation of God. *Logos* is not the word Paul uses here. When he refers to the sword of the Spirit as the Word of God, he uses the word *rhema.*

Rhema does not refer to the entire Word of God but to specific passages in the Word of God. In other words, a word within *the* Word—a specific passage, place, and verse within the written revelation of God.

He's saying you need to learn how to make a precision strike with precision accuracy, matching whatever trial, temptation, or satanic affliction with the exact verse of Scripture you need to combat it.

As a member of the KCPD, we would spend hours and hours drawing our weapons before ever firing them. To prepare for an armed confrontation, your weapon must become an extension of your body, as natural in your hands as a spoon or a fork. We fired thousands of rounds under various conditions and situations. We didn't know it, but we were building "muscle memory," the neurological pathways necessary to survive a gun battle with a real-life opponent, with real bullets flying from someone who is really trying to kill you at close range.

Training was critical because in life and death situations, we don't have time to think. In fact, under extreme duress, the brain doesn't think. That's why most people just freeze up and shut down. Through training, the brain reacts without even having to think through what to do. We've already been there mentally hundreds of times before.

We became intimately familiar with our weapons and how to use them in a millisecond's notice. When the bullets start flying, it's too late to figure out what to do. That is the problem for many Christians who know little about their weapon. They haven't trained with it, and they're not ready for a confrontation with the enemy. Preparing for battle takes work!

> *Be diligent to present yourself approved to God, a worker*
> *who does not need to be ashamed...* (2 Timothy 2:15).

Here's the point: Becoming a skilled swordsman as a Kingdom warrior takes work, but it's worth it because this is war!

As an expert with the sword of the Spirit, Jesus held a clinic in Luke 4. When Jesus was tempted by the devil, He taught us exactly how to use the *rhema*—the short sword, the Word of God—by taking it out three times. Three times He was tempted, and with three precision strikes, He cut His enemy to shreds. Jesus had fasted for forty days, and Satan came to Him tempting Him to turn stones into bread. Jesus brought out His sword quoting from Deuteronomy 8:3, *"Man shall not live by bread alone."*

Next, Satan showed Jesus all the kingdoms of the world and tempted Him saying he would give them all to Him if, *"You will worship before me."* Jesus brought out His *rhema* again and with another precision strike, He withstood Satan's temptation, quoting Deuteronomy 6:13, *"You shall fear the Lord your God and serve Him."*

Finally, Satan tempted Jesus saying, *"If You are the Son of God, throw Yourself down from here."* Satan was saying, if You are really the Messiah, throw Yourself off the temple, and You will not be harmed because if You are really God, Your angels will come and capture You. Satan even twisted Scripture from Psalms, saying that God would give His angels charge over Jesus to keep Him safe. Jesus didn't hesitate. Once more He pulled out His *rhema,* His short sword, and with precision accuracy He quoted Deuteronomy 6:16, *"You shall not tempt the Lord your God."*

With three precision strikes, Jesus sent Satan into retreat. That is exactly how Paul wants us to learn to use the sword of the Spirit, using specific Scripture passages from the Word of God against your specific trial or tribulation.

CHAPTER 18

A TWO-EDGED SWORD CUTS BOTH WAYS

For the word of God is living and powerful, and sharper than any two-edged sword, piercing even to the division of soul and spirit, and of joints and marrow, and is a discerner of the thoughts and intents of the heart (Hebrews 4:12)

There were many swords in Paul's day and even in our day that only have one cutting edge, but the Bible makes it very clear that the Roman short sword is a unique two-edged sword. God uses one edge on you, and the other edge is for us to use on the principalities and powers of the adversary.

Before you were born again by faith in Jesus Christ, you came into this world physically alive but spiritually dead. You were born as a member of Adam's fallen race with Adam's fallen image and Adam's fallen nature. You had a living body, a living soul, but a dead spirit. That is why Jesus says in John 3:3, *"Most assuredly, I say to you, unless one is born again, he cannot see the kingdom of God."*

He was speaking of a spiritual birth. The moment you placed your faith in Jesus Christ, you were born again spiritually. At that moment, the Spirit of God took His Word that created you and like a surgeon's scalpel, He cut your soul free from your spirit so that your spirit could live and be at one with His Spirit. You were instantly born again spiritually.

The Spirit of God still takes the Word of God every single day, like a surgeon's scalpel, to continue cutting away those parts of your flesh that keep you from living the abundant life in Christ and becoming more like Him. Why? Because sin is like a foreign body in your life.

A few chapters back, I told you my saga of getting hit on the head with the tree limb and finding out later that I had been stitched up with half the tree still in my head. I started to suspect something was wrong because it just wouldn't heal. When I realized it was getting infected, I went back to the doctor. He said, "Yes, you have a foreign body." That's a medical term when you have something in your body that isn't supposed to be there.

Just like a foreign body causes infection, sin also is a foreign body that infects your soul. My doctor sent me to a plastic surgeon to cut out the bark that had been left under my scalp. And just in time. By the time I got to the plastic surgeon, it was already starting to sprout leaves!

Here's the point: In the same way a surgeon takes a scalpel to remove a foreign body so healing can begin, the Spirit of God uses the Word of God in your life. Not just at the moment of salvation, *"piercing even to the division of soul and spirit"* so your spirit can live, but also as a *"discerner of the thoughts and intents of the heart."*

The Word of God gets down into the very core of your being.

Jeremiah 17:9 says, *"The heart is deceitful above all things, and desperately wicked; who can know it?"* The Word of God gets down to those underlying areas of our lives that we don't even know about. It cleans us out and cleans us up so we can be healthy and holy like Him. I've had people say to me, "Phil, that sermon kind of cut deep today." They are right! The Word of God is a precise cutting instrument, and sometimes the truth cuts. For a surgeon to bring healing, a cut has to be made.

Like a highly skilled surgeon, the Spirit of God wants to cut away everything in our lives that is not of Him. He doesn't do it to hurt us; He does it to help us. Ultimately, it's to get the infection out and bring healing so we can be healthy, happy, victorious followers of Jesus Christ the way He intended since the Garden of Eden.

> You swing the "sword of the Spirit" by the "word of your testimony."

The sword of the Spirit is the single most powerful weapon in the universe. It's a supernatural two-edged weapon. You allow God to use it on you, but then you have to learn how to turn it on the adversary with precision accuracy just as Jesus did when He was tempted in the wilderness. You can see why Satan hates the Bible, why society shuns the Bible, and our culture derides the Bible. Satan knows how dangerous God's Word is in the hands of somebody who believes the Bible and knows how to use it.

You swing the sword like Jesus did through *"the word of* [your] *testimony"* according to Revelation 12:11. Through the proclamation, declaration, and verbal confession of God's Word and God's promises, you release supernatural weaponry against the enemy! When you quote the Word of God, your voice becomes the voice of God. This is the weapon that will proceed out of the mouth of the Son of God.

> *Now out of His mouth goes a sharp sword, that with it He should strike the nations...* (Revelation 19:15).

What is this sword that proceeds out of the mouth of Jesus? It's the sword of the Spirit, which is the Word of God. In the same way, Jesus will open His mouth, and by the word of His testimony, He will strike His enemies at His Second Coming. When you open your mouth to quote the Word of God, your voice becomes a sword!

When I was in the police academy, one of my instructors told us our first weapon was our voice. I didn't understand what he meant until he explained. A good officer knows how to use his voice to de-escalate situations and take control when situations are out of control. In police work, it's called "command presence." It's the ability to get people to do what you say with nothing more than the tone of your voice's commands. It's how you walk and it's how you talk. It's not about how loudly you speak but how you speak.

Normally people who are yelling and screaming aren't in control. They are out of control. Satan is not intimidated by how loudly you speak. But he is intimidated by how you speak. When you speak forth the Word of God, your voice becomes a weapon in the hands of the Spirit of God.

> When you quote the Word of God, your voice becomes a sword!

This training came in handy one night on the streets of Kansas City. Through the blackness of the night, I had chased a guy who was wanted for a crime. I caught him in the backyard of a house. Unfortunately, I had taken my radio off my belt while riding in the squad car because it was in the way of my seatbelt. Normally I had time to put it back on my belt before getting out of the car, but this time everything went down too fast. I jumped out of the car without retrieving my radio. I quickly realized my partner didn't know where I was. I was alone with no way of calling for backup. I could hear the police helicopter somewhere overhead, but the pilot hadn't seen me.

Then things started to get scary. The guy I arrested clearly had some friends or family in the house, and he was trying to get in through the back door when I caught him. I now had him under arrest when suddenly the back door of the house flew open, and a bunch of very large men came pouring out into the backyard. They weren't coming to invite me in for a cappuccino, and they were clearly not "officer friendly." In fact, they made it clear they were "officer enemies."

They were surrounding me and closing in. I knew I was in trouble and quickly thought of my options. There were way too many of them and only one of me. I couldn't just unload my gun on them, not yet anyway. So I unloaded my voice on them. My command presence caught them off guard. I began commanding them with a clear, calm, and confident voice.

They momentarily backed down. I wasn't screaming, but I was speaking loudly and confidently. I think I made them wonder if I was a little bit crazy. It took them by surprise and made them pause long enough to rethink their next move. I knew I was going to get my backside kicked or maybe worse, but my voice had been enough to make them pause to reconsider and hold them off long enough for my buddies to locate me. I was never so happy to see two of my SWAT brothers come around the corner into the backyard.

> As a child of God, you carry Kingdom power and authority!

Your voice is a weapon. When you use your voice to proclaim God's Word, your voice becomes God's voice. Your voice becomes a supernatural sword in the hands of the Holy Spirit. And your enemy must retreat.

> *They overcame him* [Satan] *by the blood of the Lamb and by the word of their testimony...*" (Revelation 12:11).

As a child of God, you carry Kingdom authority, having been redeemed by the blood of Calvary. You are armed with supernatural weaponry, which is the word of your testimony.

It's no wonder Satan wants you to doubt and disbelieve the Bible as God's Word. If you don't believe it, it becomes just a book with no bullets. He wants to disarm you because he doesn't want you to be a threat to his kingdom or the principalities and powers that want to control you.

Here's the point: God has armed us for victory and not defeat. With the Word of God in our hands and in our hearts, we are armed and dangerous.

Satan will go to any lengths to discredit the Bible, causing doubt and disbelief about God's Word. It is the only way he can disarm Christians and disarm the Church. It is the Word of God that has the power to destroy him and from which he must retreat. It was the Word of God that spoke light into the darkness, and it's still the Word of God that speaks light into the darkness of our world.

John 1:1 says it all: *"In the beginning was the Word, and the Word was with God, and the Word was God."* John 1:14 continues, *"And the Word became flesh and dwelt among us...."*

The Bible is the written Word, but Jesus is the Living Word. It's the Word of God that destined Him to one day be crucified on the cross as the Lamb of God slain from the foundations of the earth. It was the Word of God that three days later brought Jesus back from the dead and brought Him up from the grave. It's the Word of God that one day will destroy all of God's enemies at the Second Coming of Christ.

CHAPTER 19

Time to Go on the Offensive

Now I saw heaven opened, and behold, a white horse. And He who sat on him was called Faithful and True, and in righteousness He judges and makes war. His eyes were like a flame of fire, and on His head were many crowns. He had a name written that no one knew except Himself. He was clothed with a robe dipped in blood, and His name is called The Word of God. And the armies in heaven, clothed in fine linen, white and clean, followed Him on white horses. Now out of His mouth goes a sharp sword, that with it He should strike the nations. And He Himself will rule them with a rod of iron. He Himself treads the winepress of the fierceness and wrath of Almighty God (Revelation 19:11-15).

The Bible is the Word of God, and with that one word, He is going to put down all powers and principalities. He's going to defeat Satan and all of His enemies, and He's going to take back the stolen territory called earth.

When all that takes place, the war for the world is going to be over, including the war for the world that you and I are even now part of, all with one word! Verse 15 says about Jesus, *"Now out of His mouth goes a sharp sword."* A sharp sword is going to proceed forth from His mouth with one word. The same word that created everything you see is the very same word that's going to pull down all principalities, all powers, and all demonic authorities. As children of God, we have the very same sword as *the* Son of God so that we can take back enemy territory and enemy ground.

Remember, in warfare the objective is to take ground away from the enemy. Whichever army takes the most ground eventually wins the war. Our goal as Christians should be to have an *advance mentality*. Yes, God has given us defensive armor so we can defend the high ground, but we cannot win if all we ever do is defend. Eventually, you have to get off the defensive and get on the offensive.

Whether defending or advancing, you do it by standing. You defend the high ground by standing on the finished work of the Living Word and the promises of the written Word. You swing your sword in exactly the same way—by standing on the finished work of the Living Word and the promises of the written Word. Remember what Paul says, *"stand fast!"* The way you swing the Word of God is by standing on the Word of God.

Here's the point: God has given us the Word of God, the sword of the Spirit, not only to defend God's territory but to take new territory and take back stolen territory.

Jesus said Satan is a thief who comes to steal, kill, and destroy. Many Christians have allowed Satan to have authority over their marriage. Perhaps you have given ground to the enemy, and your marriage is on the rocks even though the One who has all power and authority won that ground. Now you are wondering if your marriage is going to make it. It's time to take back that stolen ground from the enemy.

There are others in complete bondage to their thoughts and enslaved by their feelings. Satan has assaulted the high ground of our mind and emotions, causing us to give up the ground of our mind. Because we've given up the high ground of our mind, he controls our lives, and it is time to take back stolen ground from the enemy. It's time to attach bayonets, pull out your sword, and charge into the face of the enemy.

ASSAULT—COUNTER ASSAULT

In warfare, when one side makes an assault, there has to be a counter-assault. Every time we come under the assault of the enemy, we have to counter with an assault of our own. In the same way that Jesus countered Satan's assault, we have to learn to counter Satan's assault. You counter Satan's assault of lies and deception, evil thoughts and fantasies, trials, temptations, and tribulations in the very same way Jesus did—with the Word of God. Our weapon is belief in the written Word and obedience to the Living Word.

If you don't want to be taken captive by the enemy and you don't want your family to be taken captive, you have to learn how to counter Satan's lies and deception with the Word of God. There is no amount of counseling, psychology, sociology, and no amount of human philosophy that can counter Satan's demonic power and authority. The Word of God is the only weapon that can pull down the supernatural stronghold he has in your life because it is a supernatural weapon!

Here's the point: If you will believe the written Word and obey the Living Word, you can take any ground away from the enemy. It doesn't matter how strong that stronghold may be.

It is important for you to understand that faith in what God has said is the trigger that unleashes divine power. If you don't believe it, don't bother swinging it. You can say it, you can quote it, you can know it—but if you don't believe it, the enemy has already disarmed you.

In the heat of spiritual combat, you must be able to instantly choose to believe what God has said, regardless of what you see. If you already believe the Word of God, you won't have to even pause to consider any other option. Satan defeats you by getting you to believe the things you see instead of believing what God has said. It is faith in what God has said that unleashes the divine power that can pull down every stronghold.

> Faith in God's Word unleashes divine power to pull down every stronghold.

If he can deceive you into putting your faith in the circumstances and situations you can see instead of putting your faith in what God has said, you are losing ground and on the way to destruction. Eve fell because she failed to counter what Satan said with what God said. She misquoted what God spoke to her, she didn't stand on God's word, she didn't believe God's word; consequently, she quickly fell to the enemy.

Jesus, when tempted by the very same serpent in the very same way, through *"the lust of the flesh, the lust of the eyes, and the pride of life"* (1 John 2:16), pulled out His sword. He countered that assault with an assault of His own. Three times Jesus said, *"It is written."* He cut His enemy to shreds, and Satan had to retreat.

As Christians, we win in the very same way with the Word of God. We stand on the high ground of what God has said and what Christ has done. You must know what God says, believe what God says, and then proclaim what God says. Proclaim God's Word just as Jesus proclaimed it. In every situation, learn to do what Jesus did when assaulted with an enemy temptation and enemy affliction.

The written Word of God, when spoken aloud into a specific situation with the Holy Spirit's inspiration and authority, becomes an indefensible weapon against the enemy. Speak the promises of God and proclaim the Word of God specifically into whatever trial, tribulation, or affliction you face. Remember, the sword of the Spirit is a short sword used for close combat. You need to get to the place where you declare the Word of God over your situation without having to think about it because you have spent valuable time reading and absorbing it.

The Church in the United States is largely powerless against the enemy because Satan has disarmed it. Eighty percent of churches in America no longer view the Bible as the authoritative Word of God. They have a cut-and-paste theology that has led to weak and anemic Christianity! What was meant to be the giver of life can now only help dead people stay dead! They have a form of godliness but deny its power (2 Timothy 3:5).

The moment you doubt what God has said, you lay down your sword. Satan has disarmed you. When you doubt the authority of the Bible, the reliability of the Bible, the inerrancy of the Bible, the infallibility of the Bible, you give ground to the enemy, you give Satan the high ground, and you take a position of defeat.

This is why the Bible is the most attacked book in American and world history. It is the most attacked book by our culture and our society. Churches all across this nation no longer believe in its authority. It is simply a book of good ideas. Many believe it contains some good moral principles and that parts of it are the mind of God, but it's not completely the Word of God. The result is a church that has been disarmed by the enemy. A church that is putting its hope in the methods and models of humans and philosophies is utterly powerless against the enemy.

Here's the point: When you doubt the Word of God, you quench the Spirit of God. When you quench the Spirit of God, you lose the power of God, and without the power of God, you have no hope of defeating demonic powers and authorities.

I made the decision a long time ago to put my hope, faith, and destiny in God's eternal Word, the Bible. Maybe you haven't made that decision yet, and I hope that you will. Multiplied millions down through the ages have made that decision. We have examined the evidence, and we believe in the infallibility, reliability, and authority of Scripture.

> We have the most powerful supernatural weapon in the universe, but far too many simply don't know enough about it to use it.

Perhaps it's not that you don't necessarily believe the Word of God, but rather you don't know your weapon well enough to use it.

Any weapon is only as good as the hands that hold it. My handgun on the KCPD was a Smith and Wesson 4026. It was a .40 caliber that held twelve rounds. It was a good combat pistol, but most importantly, I knew how to use it. I trained with it for so long it became an extension of my arm. But the first time I fired a fully automatic submachine gun, it wasn't pretty. It was downright embarrassing. I would have been lucky to hit the side of a barn! That weapon in my hands wasn't a real threat to the enemy yet because I wasn't trained. If you're untrained, it's the same as being unarmed.

Far too many Christians either don't bring their weapons or don't know how to use them. Satan disarmed them by doubt or disbelief. Others believe the Word of God, but they don't really know it well enough to use it because they simply won't do the hard work of studying it.

There's a reason why years ago as a member of the police academy, after we were issued our guns and before they ever let us shoot them, we sat in a classroom all day long taking them apart and putting them back together again. We were educated about all the individual parts and how they worked. I didn't think I needed to know how the gun worked. I didn't even want to know how it worked. I just wanted to get out there and shoot it, but our instructors knew what they were doing.

GOD'S WORD IS LIFE-SAVING

In the heat of combat, you need to be so familiar with your weapon and its intricacies, not just outside but even inside, that it becomes an extension of your person. The point of that weapon wasn't to go target shooting and have fun. The point of it was to save my life. God has given you a weapon for the very same purpose.

Satan is not in the least bit intimidated if you have in your home a big family Bible placed in the middle of your coffee table. He's not impressed by how big your Bible is if you don't know and believe what's in it.

> *Be diligent to present yourself approved to God, a worker who does not need to be ashamed, rightly dividing the word of truth* (2 Timothy 2:15).

We live in a Laodicean age. The Laodiceans were Christians who were lukewarm. They were spiritually apathetic and spiritually complacent. We want everything to come easy. "Make it easy for me, preacher, just give me enough little bite-sized pieces to get through the week. Don't go too deep! I might have to think."

In Second Timothy 2:15, Paul was telling Timothy, his son in the faith, to be a worker of the Word. It takes work if you are going to know it well enough to use it. It's going to take effort. The Bible is not meant only to be read, it's meant to be studied.

We live in a culture where people are constantly wrongly dividing the Word of Truth, taking it out of context, twisting it, and contorting it. Satan just loves it! Study God's Word and believe it.

If you are going to beat back the enemy and take new ground and new territory, you also have to memorize God's Word. In the heat of the moment, you may not always have your concordance, and there's no time to say, "Now wait a minute, time out, I have to find this verse. I have a concordance so I have one word…let's see, it's here somewhere."

When you're under fire from the enemy, you need to be able to quote God's Word. This is where people start rolling their eyes. I hear people all the time say, "Phil, I just can't memorize Scripture." They say they can't memorize the Bible because they are horrible at memorization. That's not true.

You must believe the Word, study the Word, and memorize the Word!

You have memorized things in your life you didn't even try to memorize such as where you live and how to get home every day. You have memorized your phone number, social security number, home address, email address, somebody else's email address, and phone number. You can memorize. You have memorized jingles from songs that were popular years ago. You can still recite them. You have memorized things that don't have nearly as much importance as what the Bible says.

Many years ago, McDonald's was trying to promote their Big Macs, and they came up with a little jingle. If you are my age or older, you still remember it even though it was years ago. "Two all-beef patties, special sauce, lettuce, cheese, pickles, onions on a sesame seed bun." You still remember it—that's long-term memory.

Don't just memorize God's Word, meditate on it. Process it, pray over it, and actually digest it. To meditate on the Word means more than you just getting into the Word of God—it's letting the Word of God get into you.

CHAPTER 20

GOD'S WINNING STRATEGY

This Book of the Law shall not depart from your mouth, but you shall meditate in it day and night, that you may observe to do according to all that is written in it. For then you will make your way prosperous, and then you will have good success (Joshua 1:8).

When Joshua, the great military general of the Hebrews, was crossing over the Jordan, he was making a military conquest for the Promised Land. In Joshua 1, he was going against an army and race of giants with fortified cities. You would think, as he's getting ready to lead his army across the Jordan River, that God would talk to him about military strategy—how to divide his army or how to attack those fortified cities. God says none of that.

The military strategy God gave him is recorded in Joshua 1:8. God talked to Joshua about the Book of the Law, and He said it *"shall not depart from your mouth, but you shall meditate in it day and night, that you may observe to do according to all that is written in it. For then you will make your way prosperous, and then you will have good success."*

That is the real prosperity theology. You hear a lot about prosperity theology in our day, about how you come to Jesus and you will be rich, thin, healthy, and wealthy. You'll never get sick, and you'll never have a problem. But Jesus said if you want to come after Him, you are going to have to deny yourself and pick up your cross. That doesn't sound like prosperity theology. It's not self-enhancement, it's self-denial.

Warfare is hard. If you want to win, it's going to cost you. The key to success is a winning military strategy like the one God gave Joshua. If you are going to defeat the enemy and take new ground and new territory, you have to obey the Word of God. Satan does not care how much of the Bible you can quote and or how much you know if you will not obey it! Satan can quote more Scripture in the next nanosecond than you and I could quote together in the next year. He knows the Bible. He does not care how theologically sound you are or how doctrinally deep you are.

Satan knows what it says, and he knows how to apply it. He just doesn't want *you* to apply it. Every time you disobey the Word of God, you are giving ground to the enemy and giving away God's territory. When you submit to Christ's authority, He promises a life of victory and power and liberty. Disobedience is always two steps backward: it's giving back ground that Jesus has won in your life.

When you stop submitting to Christ's authority, you automatically start submitting to Satan's authority. When you were submitted to sin, you were submitted to Satan, and you were giving ground to the enemy.

Here's the point: Whether you want to take back ground in your marriage, with your children, in your thought life, or some habit or addiction, the answer is the same—obey God's Word.

Every time you disobey the Word of God, you take one step back and give ground to the enemy. Ephesians 4:27 says don't give place to the devil. He lost his place in your life as a born-again, blood-bought child of God. When you disobey God, you give place to the devil. If you want to take it back, you must fix your bayonet on the Word and go on the offensive by becoming a doer of the Word of God.

Satan has had a play day and a hay day in the marriages of some believers, even though they are born-again, blood-bought children of God. You were born again to live abundantly and have a marriage of joy and love and intimacy. The reason you are not is you haven't obeyed God's instruction in Ephesians 5:21-33 for husbands and wives. That's it! "We just don't communicate well, we just don't understand each other, we need to go to a counselor, we need…"

Every time you sin, you retreat and give Satan territory.

It doesn't do any good to know God's Word and quote it if you won't obey it. This is warfare, and that means somebody is going to win and somebody is going to lose. Sin gives ground to the enemy.

Every time you sin, you retreat and give Satan territory. When you obey, you take back that ground.

Remember the words of the apostle Paul in Second Corinthians 10:5: *"Casting down arguments and every high thing that exalts itself against the knowledge of God."* There's the assault, and the second part of that same verse is your counterassault: *"Bringing every thought into captivity to the obedience of Christ."* The NIV says it this way: *"We demolish arguments and every pretension that sets itself up against the knowledge of God, and we take captive every thought to make it obedient to Christ."*

Paul ends verse 6 with these words, *"...being ready to punish all disobedience when your obedience is fulfilled."* Paul is saying it's time to take revenge on sin and punish sin. He is saying take no prisoners, declare war on sin, fix bayonets, charge into the enemy, and take back some territory.

This is warfare, and in warfare there are no rules. If I have an addiction to pornography and I just can't stop it, I'm going to throw my computer out the window. I'm going to get a flip phone so I don't have Internet access if that's what it takes to win. If I have an illicit attraction to someone who is not my spouse, I'm not going to throw them out the window, but I'm going as far as I can in the opposite direction when I see the person coming my way. I'm going to tell a trusted friend to pray for me and provide accountability.

Resist the devil and he WILL flee.

I'm not giving ground to the enemy. I realize what that means for me. If I have given up ground to the enemy in my thoughts and my emotions, that means I'm going to choose to believe what God has said no matter what I feel. I'm going to believe in the truth of God's Word.

- Romans 8:37 says I am more than a conqueror.
- John 10:10 says I can live abundantly.
- Second Corinthians 2:14 says I can live triumphantly.

There are days when I don't feel very triumphant. There are days when I'm tired; there are days when I'm exhausted emotionally and mentally. I get down, depressed, and dejected. I know exactly what you go through, and I can tell you there's no magic potion, no magic Bible verse. It's simply choosing to live what God has said.

I can choose to be joyful even when I'm going through a time that's sorrowful. Satan, you are not going to win. I am what the Bible says I am. I have what the Bible says I have. Satan, you will not win. I will do whatever it takes to punish sin because God has given me weapons, and I can win!

You can win too! God is on your side—He has provided every defensive and offensive weapon you need to be victorious every day of your life.

PART IX

THE WARRIOR'S PRAYER

Praying always with all prayer and supplication in the Spirit, being watchful to this end with all perseverance and supplication for all the saints—and for me, that utterance may be given to me, that I may open my mouth boldly to make known the mystery of the gospel, for which I am an ambassador in chains; that in it I may speak boldly, as I ought to speak (Ephesians 6:18-20).

The 19th-century pastor and theologian E.M. Bounds said, "Prayer doesn't just prepare us for the battle. *Prayer is the battle.*" The apostle Paul, a 1st-century pastor and theologian, said something similar when he summarized this great field manual on spiritual warfare saying, *"Pray always."* Every day, learn to get out of bed and dress for the day by putting on the armor of God, *"praying always with all prayer and supplication in the Spirit..."* (Ephesians 6:18).

Here's the point: You cannot live in spiritual victory apart from learning how to pray with a warfare mentality. You can pray anytime, anywhere. Paul does not equate a piece of the Roman armor to prayer, but it is nonetheless essential for victory against all the power of the enemy.

You don't dress for combat spiritually the way you dress for combat physically. There is no helmet of salvation that you can physically put on and take off. Physically, every piece of armor represents what God has given us spiritually. You don't put on literal, physical armor; you put on spiritual armor through prayer. It is essential that we learn how to pray because it is prayer that makes all the armor of God operable and powerful in our lives.

> Prayer makes all the armor of God operable and powerful in our lives.

You strap on the sword of the Spirit through prayer, you put on the helmet of salvation through prayer, and you put on the breastplate of righteousness through prayer. In this final part of *The Weapons of Our Warfare*, I pray you are becoming thoroughly convinced that your prayers affect the warfare in the heavenlies between the angels of God and the angels of Satan as they wage war over the world and the affairs of humankind.

Daniel 10 illustrates this powerful truth perhaps better than anywhere else in Scripture. The prophet Daniel was a genuine Kingdom warrior and prayer warrior. Daniel 10 is an illustration in the Old Testament of why we should do exactly what Paul says in Ephesians 6:18: *"praying always with all prayer and supplication in the Spirit, being watchful to this end with all perseverance and supplication for all the saints."*

Paul says we should pray always as he closes out this dissertation on spiritual warfare and the armor of God. He says don't forget to do this because our prayers intersect with angelic activities, both good and evil. Daniel 10 provides us a window to see what happens behind the scenes in the unseen spiritual realm when you pray.

Historically, Daniel is in Babylonian captivity. He's a Jew who was born in Jerusalem. In 605 BC, King Nebuchadnezzar and the Babylonian army pillaged and conquered Jerusalem. The Babylonian Empire emerged as the world power at that time, and they carried the choice Hebrew children back to Babylon. Daniel was just a teenager when he was taken into captivity, but in Daniel 10, he is an old man having spent most of his life in Babylon.

The Babylonian Empire had risen and fallen, and the Medo-Persian Empire had now risen. Daniel realized, based on Scripture, that the captivity of the Jews was now coming to an end. The biblical and historical records tell us King Cyrus of Persia had finally decreed that the Jews could go back to Jerusalem. No longer did they have to live in captivity.

Daniel was mourning and he began to pray. Although the Jews could finally go back to their homeland, nobody really wanted to go. You see, Daniel was living in a time much like ours today—a time of spiritual apathy and spiritual complacency. The Jews had become used to living in captivity, and Daniel mourned for his nation and his people. He began praying that revival would come to his nation and to his generation.

Daniel 10:1-4 tells us:

In the third year of Cyrus king of Persia a message was revealed to Daniel, whose name was called Belteshazzar. The message was true, but the appointed time was long;

and he understood the message, and had understanding of the vision. In those days I, Daniel, was mourning three full weeks. **I ate no pleasant food, no meat or wine came into my mouth, nor did I anoint myself at all, till three whole weeks were fulfilled.** *Now on the twenty-fourth day of the first month as I was by the side of the great river, that is, the Tigris....*

Daniel prayed and fasted for his people for three weeks. He did not bathe, he did not eat, he did not drink. He was on his face before God praying and fasting, day and night.

As Christians, we often say things like, "God needs to send revival to our nation. God, send revival to America. God, send revival to our generation." The real question is, "Do we really mean it and do we really want it?" Daniel wanted it so badly he prayed and fasted around the clock for three weeks.

Many Christians, especially in the United States, can't pray for three minutes, much less three weeks. Consequently, other than perhaps the Jesus Movement of the 1970s, real widespread revival hasn't come to our nation for more than one hundred years. We slowly die inwardly of our spiritual apathy and spiritual complacency, falling deeper and deeper into moral depravity and spiritual anarchy as a society.

Daniel understood that if revival was to come and if God was going to do something special and supernatural in his nation, he was going to have to fast and pray before Him. Even though they could go back to Jerusalem and rebuild their city and their way of life and worship the God of heaven, he realized that nobody really cared. They had become complacent. They had settled for what they had, and tragically, nobody wanted to leave. So Daniel began to pray and fast.

Praying and fasting is not an isolated occurrence found only in the Old Testament Book of Daniel. It is found throughout the Word of God because prayer does not prepare you for the battle—prayer *is* the battle! The battle is won or lost in prayer.

Life is full of battles, and whatever battles come into your life, they are won before they are ever fought, depending on the amount of time you are willing to spend in prayer until the answer comes. For Daniel, it was three weeks. For some, it's three months or three years or even longer. Daniel was fervently praying and fasting because only then do you become a real threat to the kingdom of darkness as a child of the Light. You become a threat to the kingdom of Satan as a member of the Kingdom of God.

> *Now this is the confidence that we have in Him, that if we ask anything according to His will, He hears us* (1 John 5:14).

When we pray and fast, it moves the heart of God in heaven so that something changes on earth. God's power is released in the spiritual realm to oppose the work of demons and the work of Satan and his powers and principalities.

We see an example of the power of prayer and fasting recorded by Matthew, Mark, and Luke. The disciples were casting out demons, and one day they came to a little boy who was possessed by a demon. It was an unclean spirit, and they could not cast it out. They had cast out other unclean spirits, but they could not cast this one out.

Jesus came along and cast out the demon. Then the disciples looked at Jesus and said, "Why could we not cast it out?" Jesus looked at them and said, *"This kind does not go out except by prayer and fasting"* (Matthew 17:21).

Jesus was teaching the disciples that prayer and fasting break satanic strongholds and demonic attacks. It is the vehicle God has chosen for the release of His power into your life over sin, over Satan, and over every stronghold. After Daniel had prayed and fasted for three weeks, somebody showed up in Daniel 10:5-9. Daniel says:

> *I lifted my eyes and looked, and behold, a certain man clothed in linen, whose waist was girded with gold of Uphaz! His body was like beryl, his face like the appearance of lightning, his eyes like torches of fire, his arms and feet like burnished bronze in color, and the sound of his words like the voice of a multitude. And I, Daniel, alone saw the vision, for the men who were with me did not see the vision; but a great terror fell upon them, so that they fled to hide themselves. Therefore I was left alone when I saw this great vision, and no strength remained in me; for my vigor was turned to frailty in me, and I retained no strength. Yet I heard the sound of his words; and while I heard the sound of his words I was in a deep sleep on my face, with my face to the ground.*

This passage records a description of the preincarnate Lord Jesus Christ. It was Christ Himself who came and appeared to Daniel centuries before He would be born of a virgin in Bethlehem and laid in a manger.

Remember who Jesus is and never forget. He is more than just a son of God. He is the eternal, sinless Son of God. He is the second Person of the Trinity. He has always existed. He is from everlasting to everlasting, and He is deity. He was the Word of God who walked with Adam in the Garden in the cool of the day in Genesis 3, long before the Word of God *"became flesh and dwelt among us"* according to John 1:14.

Jesus appears in the Old Testament at strategic places throughout human history. When you compare this description in Daniel with the description in Revelation 1:14-15, as John the revelator is transported into the presence of Jesus Christ in heaven, they are almost identical: *"His eyes like a flame of fire; His feet were like fine brass."*

In Daniel 10:7, there were other men with Daniel, but they didn't see what Daniel saw, and they didn't hear what Daniel heard. When Jesus spoke, it sounded like thunder to them. We see the same thing in the book of Acts with Saul on the road to Damascus. When Jesus appeared to Saul, he saw Jesus, but the other men just saw a bright light. Saul heard the words of Jesus, but the other men said it sounded like thunder.

You can be very close to God and still be very far away.

There were men in the presence of God, but when God spoke, they didn't hear. When God showed up, they didn't see Him. There are two types of people in every church on any given Sunday morning. There are those who get it and those who don't have the foggiest idea about what is going on. When the Word of God is spoken, there are those who hear the voice of God, but there are others who never, ever hear the voice of God. They never hear God because you do not hear God with your ears, you hear God with your heart.

If your heart is not humble and open to hearing the voice of God, it doesn't matter how many times you read the Word of God or how many times you hear the Word of God. If your heart is not humble and open, you will not hear the voice of God.

Here were men who heard the voice of God, and it just sounded like thunder to them. That is the very same reason why many so-called Christians can go to church week in and week out and leave completely unchanged and untouched, while somebody sitting next to them can hear the very same message and leave transformed. The difference is not the message; the difference is you and what's in you.

Daniel 10:9 continues after Jesus came on the scene: *"Yet I heard the sound of his words; and while I heard the sound of his words I was in a deep sleep on my face, with my face to the ground."*

Have you ever heard somebody say, "Wow, God just blew me away!" Daniel is blown away. If you get in the presence of Jesus Christ, you are going to get blown away as well. Daniel is face down, and he fainted.

You don't have to imagine what's going to happen. Someday we're going to get in the presence of Jesus. When you get in the presence of Jesus Christ, you too are going to be face down, prostrate on the ground. You won't be able to move, you won't be able to speak, and you won't be able to say a thing. "Well, when I get to heaven, I'm going to ask God…" No, you won't. You will be face down in the presence of God. Then God is going to stand you up, and there will be singing, shouting, dancing, and celebrating.

The first time you come into the presence of our God, you will be face down just like Daniel. You'll be blown away, just as Daniel was blown away. He faints, but somebody else comes and wakes him up. It is not Jesus but an angelic being.

Daniel 10:10-12 tells us:

> *Suddenly, a hand touched me, which made me tremble on my knees and on the palms of my hands. And he said*

to me, "O Daniel, man greatly beloved, understand the words that I speak to you, and stand upright, for I have now been sent to you." While he was speaking this word to me, I stood trembling. Then he said to me, "Do not fear, Daniel, for from the first day that you set your heart to understand, and to humble yourself before your God, your words were heard; and I have come because of your words."

When you give yourself to prayer and fasting, you enter into intergalactic warfare. You see, your prayer life is really a gauge of your spiritual life and how near you can walk with God. Little prayer, little power; much prayer, much power. You want to be near God so you spend time in prayer with God. If you don't spend time in prayer with God, you will find yourself distanced from God.

Daniel spent twenty-one days in prayer. No wonder Jesus immersed him in His presence. An angelic being came and woke him up. This angelic being proceeded to describe intergalactic warfare that took place in the heavenlies as this angel came down to earth. He was accosted and held hostage by another angel.

CHAPTER 21

REAL-LIFE EXTRATERRESTRIALS

And as it was in the days of Noah, so it will be also in the days of the Son of Man (Luke 17:26).

Years ago, Hollywood released a movie entitled *E.T.* It was one of the iconic movies of the 1980s. (Here I go dating myself again!) But regardless of your age, you've probably heard of it. It was about an extraterrestrial from somewhere in outer space that crash-landed on our planet and befriended a group of boys. The movie was about helping E.T. get home. Who can ever forget the line, "E.T., phone home."

That was just a movie and entirely make-believe. But what is not make-believe is the fact that there is intelligent life out there. They are angelic beings described in Daniel 10. This angelic being tells Daniel in Daniel 10:13, *"But the prince of the kingdom of Persia withstood me twenty-one days; and behold, Michael, one of the chief princes, came to help me, for I had been left alone there with the kings of Persia."*

It is from the heavenlies that the powers and principalities—the demonic authorities that Paul writes about in Ephesians 6:12—plan their assault upon the earth against you and me. These are the real-life extraterrestrials. It's not the intelligent kind of life the average UFO enthusiast is looking for. No little green men from Mars.

Rather, they are what Paul writes about in Ephesians 6:12: *"For we do not wrestle against flesh and blood, but against principalities, against powers, against the rulers of the darkness of this age, against spiritual hosts of wickedness in the heavenly places* [the second heaven].*"*

Remember, Lucifer was thrown out of the third heaven into the second heaven. It's in the second heaven, the "heavenly places" or outer space, where Satan dwells as the *"prince of the power of the air"* (Ehpesians 2:2).

Daniel is describing the spiritual wickedness in heavenly places that Paul writes about in Ephesians 6:12, intelligent, angelic life—both good and evil. There is so much UFO hysteria in our day, from the secular news media, the History Channel, pop culture, Hollywood movies, and TV sitcoms. It makes perfect sense when one considers what is really going on in the heavenlies.

In Genesis 6, we are told about this intelligent life—the demonic beings who came down to earth and cohabitated among humans. In Luke 17:26, Jesus says, *"And as it was in the days of Noah, so it will be also in the days of the Son of Man."* Jesus was saying that the closer it gets to His Second Coming, our world is going to look more and more like it did in the days of Noah. In Genesis 6, the "gods" from the heavenlies came to earth. We are seeing prophecy fulfilled before our very eyes. Rational, educated human beings are believing more and more there has to be intelligent life in the heavenlies.

Every ancient culture—from any generation of antiquity, from any continent—has in their oral tradition a story of the gods coming down from the heavenlies, cohabitating with people on earth, and then going back. It really has happened. Genesis 6 is a historical, biblical record of the oral tradition of those ancient people.

OUTER SPACE BATTLEFIELD

Daniel 10 describes for us that outer space is a battlefield between the angels of God and the angels of Satan, the forces of God and the forces of Satan. It is intergalactic warfare between good and evil angelic beings who engage in real warfare—a war for the world.

In Daniel 10:20, the angel finished talking to Daniel, and said he was going back to heaven (the third heaven): *"Then he said, 'Do you know why I have come to you? And now I must return to fight with the prince of Persia; and when I have gone forth, indeed the prince of Greece will come.'"*

Here we catch a glimpse of the warfare that takes place in the heavenlies that impacts the affairs of us on earth. This passage teaches there are demonic princes who have power over the nations. What the Bible calls the second heaven is a battlefield in outer space. The battle is on earth and beyond earth.

In Daniel 10:13, this angel said he fought against the prince of Persia, not the physical prince, but a demonic prince. At that particular time in history, the Persians were the ruling superpower of the world. They would have another two hundred years of being the absolute world power before the Greek empire would emerge. This godly angel told Daniel he was on the way from the first day Daniel began to pray. He was intercepted by this prince of Persia and held there for twenty-one days until Michael, a stronger angel, came to assist him so he could proceed to answer Daniel's prayer.

The purpose of these demonic princes is to advance Satan's kingdom and oppose God's Kingdom in whatever part of the world Satan has assigned them. There was a demonic prince reigning over the kingdom of Persia; but already in verse 20, God's angel says that before he can go back into heaven, he will have to *"fight with the prince of Persia; and when I have gone forth, indeed the prince of Greece will come."* He is not talking about Alexander the Great who was the physical prince of the Greek empire. He's speaking of the demonic prince. He's saying once I go back into heaven, the prince of Greece is going to come.

The Greeks would not emerge as a world empire for another two hundred years at the time Daniel was writing. Alexander the Great would not be born for another two hundred years. But the angel is saying that already, two hundred years before anything on earth happens, there is warfare in the heavenlies between angelic beings and Satan's beings over what will eventually become the Grecian empire. The angel mentions this prince of Greece because that is who will empower the earthly prince, Alexander the Great.

Every war that has ever been fought historically between human beings has first been fought between angelic beings. Everything that happens on earth is but a shadow or a reflection of something that has gone on in the heavenlies.

There is a reason that for decades the entire world has been glued to the Middle East and Jerusalem, the epicenter of Christianity in particular. There's a reason there is so much crisis, chaos, war, and bloodshed in that real estate. That particular part of the globe is already destined by God to be front and center as He brings about His plan and climax for the ages—the Second Coming of Christ.

Already, the geopolitical scene is being put into place, and the props and players are being positioned for our Lord's return for His Church.

If you believe the Bible, what Daniel is writing is not allegorical, it's not symbolic, it's not figurative—it's real! God said it exactly the way He meant it. There are powers and demonic principalities over every single nation, for no other reason than to control those earthly kingdoms so God's Kingdom cannot be advanced.

DEMONIC HATRED

Who will ever forget the name Osama bin Laden? He, of course, was the founder of Al-Qaeda, the Islamic terrorist organization. He is also the mastermind of the attack on the Twin Towers in New York City, which took place on September 11, 2001. More than three thousand innocent Americans were murdered for no other reason than the hatred of a man they had never even met.

Have you ever asked yourself why he hated us so much? What did we do against him that he would hate us? There is no way to answer that logically. There is no natural explanation for that kind of nonsensical hatred. The answer can only be found in the supernatural. Bin Laden was merely flesh and blood. We have learned that we *do not wrestle against flesh and blood.* The real enemy and the source of his hatred was an enemy no one could see. Osama bin Laden was only a puppet of the real enemy—a powerful demonic principality that was pulling his strings.

He wanted to see Israel wiped off the map, along with the destruction of Western civilization, but this hatred goes much deeper than a man. Satan sees Israel and Western civilization, which historically is Judeo-Christian, as a threat to his kingdom.

It is the same reason so many like bin Laden utterly hate the Jews and want to destroy the nation of Israel. It is also the reason the

Jewish people have been the most persecuted people throughout all of history, for all of humanity. Satan hates them because they are God's chosen people by covenant. God chose to bring forth the promised Seed of Genesis 3:15 through the Jewish people. We have a Jewish Redeemer and Savior, and that is why Satan hates the Jews and so many of the nations do as well.

Satan hates the West because the Western Hemisphere is where Christianity and the Kingdom of God have advanced, gained a foothold, and gained influence. It's from here that the gospel has been taken to nations and people who never before heard the name of Jesus. Not everything is about a physical conflict. You must begin looking at life through your spiritual eyes to see behind the scenes. It's not just about what you can see. You cannot interpret what you can see properly unless you are interpreting it through the lens of Scripture and what you cannot see—the spiritual warfare in the heavenlies to advance the kingdom of Satan versus the Kingdom of heaven.

The implication in this Scripture passage is that Iran is not the only real estate with a demonic prince—the same demonic prince known as the prince of Persia, which is now Iran in Daniel 10:20. The Greeks have had a demonic prince as have every other nation from antiquity to the 21st century. Satan will control the kingdoms of this world until the true King returns, and one day soon He will.

CHAPTER 22

WHEREVER GOD MARCHES, SATAN OPPOSES

But the prince of the kingdom of Persia withstood me twenty-one days; and behold, Michael, one of the chief princes [God's archangel], came to help me, for I had been left alone there with the kings of Persia (Daniel 10:13).

I'm convinced we have demonic principalities and powers assigned to us personally, as well as our countries, cities, communities, and local church bodies. Why? Because we're advancing the gospel and the Kingdom of God, not just in our cities but worldwide. That makes us a threat to the enemy. They are there to do nothing more than oppose, hinder, and sow division and dissension among the people so he can divide and conquer. The good news is we do not have to feel threatened or fearful.

Just as Satan has angels warring *against* us, God has angels warring *for* us. There are angels all around us going to battle for us just as they did for Daniel. This particular angel was sent by God to minister to Daniel in response to his prayer, just as God does for us. The Bible says in Hebrews 1:14 that angels are *"ministering spirits sent forth to minister for those who will inherit salvation."*

The angel told Daniel he was intercepted by the demonic prince of Persia somewhere in outer space. He was accosted and held hostage. This angel was sent on a mission from God to minister to Daniel, but the demonic prince of Persia withstood him. He held up the angel and held him hostage because he opposed the work of God. Paul calls them *"principalities"* in Ephesians 6:12. The principality belonged to the prince over Persia.

God has ordered the angelic world through a structure of authority. Our prayers empower God's angels to finally overcome Satan's angels. Daniel kept praying—he didn't give up or give in. If Michael had not shown up when he did, Daniel would have continued to pray. As a result, after twenty-one days, God sent forth Michael. Verse 13 records, *"But the prince of the kingdom of Persia withstood me twenty-one days; and behold, Michael, one of the chief princes, came to help me."* God dispatched Michael, the archangel, who is far more powerful and could overcome this prince of Persia.

God has structured the angelic world through a hierarchy of authority and command. The Bible teaches there are varying levels of rank, power, and authority among the angels that cannot be usurped or lost. Although one-third of the angels rebelled with Satan, they still retained their rank.

God's angel ran into a more powerful angel of Satan of higher rank. And so God dispatched an even more powerful angel by the name of Michael who had greater rank to overcome this demonic prince so the lower-ranking angel could finally move on and complete the mission from God.

In Daniel 10, the archangel Michael, a powerful prince of the angelic host, is sent forth to overcome the prince of Persia. In Jude 9, Michael recognized Satan as the highest rank of all angels, both good and evil. Michael appears to be the highest ranking of God's angels, but Satan is still higher. God, of course, is highest and greater and more powerful than Satan and his demons.

As sons and daughters of the living God, we need to remember our Kingdom authority. Just as Michael overcame Satan by saying, *"The Lord rebuke you,"* we do the same every time we pray in Jesus' name. There is no other authority greater than the name of the Lord. Praying in the name of Jesus Christ is the starting point to learning how to pray when you are in warfare.

When you pray, appeal to the highest Authority in all of creation—Jesus Christ!

When you appeal to the authority of the name of Jesus, you are appealing to the highest Authority in the universe. You have no authority as a human being to do anything in the spiritual realm except by the authority that Christ has given to you. Our authority

WEAPONS OF OUR WARFARE

comes from Christ alone. This is why we pray in Jesus' name. It is far more than just a catchy theological tag at the end of your prayer. Jesus taught us to pray in His name because it gives you authority in the spirit realm.

Jesus says in Matthew 28:18: *"All authority has been given to Me in heaven and on earth."* The Father delegated authority to the Son, and now the Son delegates authority to us. In Luke 10:19, Jesus announced, *"Behold, I give you the authority to trample on serpents and scorpions, and over all the power of the enemy...."* Because you are in Christ, Satan no longer has authority over you—you have authority over him.

It is delegated authority, in the very same way our government delegated authority to me when I was a police officer. Before that I had no authority. Today, I have spiritual authority as a pastor, but I have no civil authority as a police officer. Today if you pull out of the parking lot and see me pull in behind you, and I put a little red light on the top of my truck and it starts spinning, you're not going to stop. I might keep after you and chase you, and you might finally pull over just because you're sick of me chasing you. You're going to say, "Phil, what are you doing? You don't have the authority to pull me over." You would be right.

I don't have the delegated authority I used to have, but a few years back, it would have been a different story. If I was in my police car and hit the red light signaling you to pull over, you would pull over because you recognize my authority.

In the very same way, Satan must now recognize your authority. Before Christ, you had no authority. You were under Satan's authority. Anyone under his authority has no option but to live in slavery and captivity. When you were born again spiritually by faith in Jesus Christ, God placed you in Christ. Positionally, you are in Him, and because you are in Him, you now wield His authority. In the very same way, you must learn how to take that authority and leverage it against Satan for you and those you love.

As a member of the police department in Kansas City, Missouri, I worked the area located next to Kansas City, Kansas. My civil authority was in Kansas City, Missouri. Once in a while, someone would make a run for Kansas City, Kansas, because the driver knew I didn't have authority once I left the municipality. If the car made it to another city, I couldn't give chase.

Here's the point: As a Christian, you need to learn where you have authority.

The moment you gave your life to Jesus, you received all power and all authority. With Satan's authority came slavery and captivity, but with Christ's authority comes liberty, victory, power, and authority. He wants you to live life abundantly.

Satan has no authority over your marriage, your home, your children, or your mind. You have the authority, and it is up to you to learn how to exercise that authority daily. If my mind wants to be captured with negative thoughts or negative emotions, I have to immediately put on the helmet of salvation. Second Corinthians 10:5 says, *"Casting down arguments and every high thing that exalts itself against the knowledge of God, bringing every thought into captivity to the obedience of Christ."*

I have lived what I am sharing with you many times over. There are days I don't feel particularly triumphant or victorious. At that moment, when Satan wants to take ground that belongs to God through my mind, my thoughts, and my emotions, I have to leverage my authority and declare:

> *Satan, you have no authority over my mind, my thoughts,*
> *or my emotions. I will not be in slavery to anxiety; I'm not*

going to live in captivity to my depression, and I'm not going to live in captivity to these negative emotions. I have been bought with a price—the blood of Jesus Christ. He has all authority over my life, and I'm not going to be captured by these negative thoughts. Satan, you are not going to win the day. My faith and hope and trust is in God Almighty, in Jesus Christ the Son of God.

You do not have to be captured by the slavery of pornography; you don't have to live in captivity to the merry-go-round of sensuality, infidelity, and immorality that so many Christians would do anything to stop. You have authority to live in liberty and to live the abundant life that Jesus came to provide for you.

Satan wants you to think you are still his slave. He wants you to think you have no options. He wants you to think you have to cave in and give in. Rather, in the heat of temptation, you exercise your authority through Jesus Christ who has all power and authority. Declare:

My life belongs to Jesus because I've been bought with a price. Satan, I will not live under the authority of pornography; I will walk away so that I can live in liberty. With his authority comes slavery, but with Christ's authority comes liberty. I will not give in, and I will not give up. I'm walking away from sin and walking toward freedom in Jesus Christ.

Satan wants you to think you have to sin, and I have written this entire book to help you understand beyond a shadow of a doubt that you do not have to sin. That doesn't mean you will never sin or that you can't sin. What it means is you have been liberated from sin and Satan. You don't have to give in—you belong to Christ.

Only when you allow Christ to have authority over you, can you exercise authority over Satan. You cannot leverage any authority over Satan if you are not allowing Jesus to have authority over you. We live in a time when people don't want to live under any authority. "I want to do my own thing and be my own boss. I'm the captain of my own ship, I can do whatever I want, and I can do it when I want. No one's going to tell me what to do." I urge you not to get too big for your britches. You can have it your way, but the moment you step out from under Christ's authority, you automatically come underneath Satan's authority—it's one or the other.

As a mortal human being, you will live under spiritual authority—it's either going to be the Savior's or it's going to be Satan's. You choose. As long as you are submitted to the authority of the Savior, you will not submit to the authority of Satan. The moment you stop submitting to Jesus' authority, you are automatically submitted to Satan. His authority will always lead you into slavery and captivity. It is a merry-go-round of insanity.

The moment you begin submitting again to Christ's authority, you take back that ground from the enemy, and you learn to leverage your authority.

CHAPTER 23

THE VALUE OF PRAYER VOLUME

Then He [Jesus] spoke a parable to them, that men always ought to pray and not lose heart (Luke 18:1).

Daniel prayed and fasted for twenty-one days straight! That's what you call volume, and it is definitely not what most of us pray. Most of us pray short, weak, watered-down 911 calls to God. "God is great, God is good, let us thank Him for this food, Amen." Satan is not threatened or intimidated by that kind of anemic prayer. It is certainly not the kind of prayer that Jesus spoke to His disciples when He told the parable of the persistent widow who never gave up. Or what Paul writes about having a combat mentality in prayer—praying with tenacity and determination where you refuse to give up and you just won't give in. Some say,

"Well, God is going to do what God is going to do. Why bother even praying? God isn't even listening, God isn't even moving."

That's exactly what Satan wants you to think because he knows the more you pray, the stronger the forces of God grow—and the weaker the forces of Satan become. He wants you to give up, and he wants you to give in. There are times in the battles of life when stress, strain, and problems put you in a fight for your life. It takes a tenacious combat mentality toward prayer to say, "I'm not giving up and I'm not giving in." That is the tenacity we need in our prayer life.

In my teenage years, when I was the picture of the prodigal son and far from God, I'm convinced my mom prayed me back to Jesus. She was a prayer warrior and intercessor. I found out years later that she had actually gone to the center of a cemetery where she worked and cried out to God on my behalf. My mom had tenacity when she prayed, and she didn't give up.

That's the kind of prayer life Paul means when he sums up his instruction on spiritual warfare in Ephesians 6:18 writing, *"Praying always."* How often? Always. How long do you do it? Always. Praying always, whatever it takes, however long it takes, with all prayer and supplication. That is true intercessory prayer for others.

Praying in the Spirit means being there in the spirit. Your mind is not wandering somewhere else. It is focused and intense—seeking God's power and provision. You don't pray with your mouth; you pray with your heart. Paul is writing about a combat mentality in which you are to persevere in prayer.

Declare: I'm not going to give up or give in. Even though it doesn't look like God is listening or God cares, I'm going to keep on keeping on.

What would have happened if Daniel had stopped praying on day 3 and thought, *Well, God isn't listening. It must mean that He doesn't care.* What would have happened if he stopped praying on day 10?

What would have happened if he would have stopped praying on day 15? We wouldn't have Daniel 10 in our Bible, and he would not have received the answer to his prayer.

> ## Praying in the Spirit means being there in the spirit.

The concept that "God is going to do whatever God is going to do" is a hyper-distortion of the doctrine of predestination that says God has already "fixed" everything. No he hasn't. In God's infinite foreknowledge, He knows all the possible outcomes of everything, but He has not predestined the outcomes.

There are some things God has fixed ahead of time and you can't change it. As a child of God, you are predestined to become like the Son of God (Romans 8:29). But that doesn't mean God has predestined every single thing in your life and there's nothing you can do to change it.

There are a lot of things God is waiting to do for you that He hasn't done yet. You are waiting on Him when He has been waiting on you. He may be waiting on you to pray, or waiting on you to ask, or waiting on you to move—to take a step toward Him in faith and obedience. It may take twenty-one days of prayer and fasting. It may take even longer. Daniel had no idea that while he was on his face praying and fasting, there was warfare going on in the heavens. At this very moment, there is so much happening that we cannot see or comprehend in the heavenly realm that is making a difference on earth.

> ## Our prayers empower the forces of good.

The way you win in any situation is through prayer. Regardless of what you see or feel, keep on praying. The old-timers used to call it praying through. You pray until you've prayed, and sometimes you have to keep praying before you really pray. That's why sometimes you pray for two minutes, look at your watch, and think it has been two hours. You are just getting started—you haven't really started to pray.

I met a family who lost a beloved son. He left home to fight in the Persian Gulf War in 1991. He survived the war and came home only to die in a car crash. His mother told me that in the face of the deepest pain and tribulation of any parent, "We learned how to pray the Word of God."

When you pray the Word of God, know that you are praying in such a way that the enemy has to retreat. This is the power of the sword of the Spirit. Satan has no counter. He has no answer, and he has no solution but to run and retreat. When you wield the sword of the Spirit in prayer, you beat back the powers of darkness and the powers of the enemy because when you pray the Word of God, you are praying the will of God.

Here's the point: When you get into the Word of God, you discover the Word of God. When you discover the Word of God, you will know the will of God.

God gave us His promise in Isaiah 55:11 that His Word would not return to Him void. God will do whatever He has said. God is not a human being—He doesn't lie (see Numbers 23:19). When God says it, it's done, and you learn to praise. This family told me when they heard the news of their son dying in a car wreck, they were as grief-stricken as anybody would be. His mother said, "We were immediately moved in our spirit to begin praising Jesus." In that moment, victory was snatched from the adversary's jaws of defeat.

Satan despises the praise of God. In the face of that tribulation or situation, no matter how hard, when you just want to give up and give in, if you will begin to praise the name of Jesus, Satan has no choice but to retreat. It's easy to praise God in the good times. When you praise Him in the hard times, what Satan wants to use for evil, God will use for good.

Satan despises the praise of God.

I want to encourage you to pray every day what I call the Warrior's Prayer. It doesn't have to be these exact words, but this is how you prepare for combat and prepare for whatever happens that day. And remember, prayer is more than preparation for the battle. Prayer *is* the battle.

> *Heavenly Father, Your warrior prepares for battle. Today I claim victory over Satan by putting on the whole armor of God. I put on the belt of truth. Now I stand firmly in the truth of Your Word so I'll not be a victim of Satan's lies. I put on the breastplate of righteousness. May it guard my heart from evil so I will remain pure and holy, protected under the blood of Jesus Christ. I put on the shoes of peace, and I stand firmly on the good news of the gospel so Your peace will shine through me and be a light to all I encounter. I take the shield of faith, and I will be ready for Satan's fiery darts of doubt, denial, and deceit so I will not be vulnerable to spiritual defeat. I put on the helmet of salvation, and I keep my mind focused on You, so Satan will not have a stronghold on my thoughts. I take the sword of the Spirit. May the two-edged sword of Your Word be ready in my hands so I can expose the tempting words of Satan. By faith, Your warrior has put on the whole armor of God. I am prepared to live this day in spiritual victory. Amen.*

In Ephesians 6, the apostle Paul is concluding his letter to the Ephesians. This is why he begins his field manual on warfare by writing, *"Finally…"* (Ephesians 6:10). He is by now a truly grizzled and scarred combat veteran. He has known many battles. Each of us will as well. Life is hard. The world is cruel. It's cursed by sin and controlled by Satan. No one goes into combat who doesn't eventually get wounded and take a hit.

Always remember, there are no blessings apart from battles. And from the greatest battles in life come the greatest blessings.

> From the greatest battles in life come the greatest blessings.

It was the fall of 1999, and I was attending a small church still in its infancy. At that time, I was a policeman and had no idea I'd ever be a pastor. My wife and I had taken our young family to this little church just looking for a place to worship. We hoped to help grow it for God's Kingdom. But things weren't going well. The church was not healthy. It was full of division, dissension, backbiting, and infighting. That is always Satan's strategy to stop the people of God—divide and conquer. He has run that play successfully over and over again throughout time.

Our pastor who had started the church resigned suddenly. It was a Tuesday night when I received a phone call from someone who served on the church's Board. They needed someone to preach on Sunday. It was hard to believe they were calling me. I was just a cop. By this time, a couple of years after joining that little church, I had already surrendered my life to full-time ministry, but I had barely started seminary. I had no formal ministry training and had only preached one or two times in my entire life. But that shows how desperate the situation was.

I thought it would be "one and done." But then I was asked to fill in the next week, and then the next week. Then I was asked to fill in until we found a full-time replacement for our pastor. I agreed.

That entire fall of 1999, I was a cop for six days out of the week and "preacher" on Sundays.

It was a very difficult time for that little church, just fighting to survive. Satan was trying to destroy it because he knew what it could become. Lots of members had already left. The morale of the church was at an all-time low. When it didn't seem like things could get any worse, it did. The one paid staff member we had left was our worship and youth pastor. He had to resign because of a moral failure in his life.

On the last Sunday of 1999, before this cop got up to preach, he had to announce that our only paid staff member was forced to resign. It was a cold winter day, and there weren't more than twenty-five adults sitting in the pews. I really thought this could be the nail in the coffin for this little church.

I don't even recall much about the sermon that day or remember much of what I said. I do remember the text was Proverbs 24:16, *"For a righteous man may fall seven times and rise again."* We are at war, and we will all take hits. You may get knocked down over and over again. But while you get knocked down, as a Kingdom warrior, you never stay down. With God's help, you get up again.

What I remember most that day was the altar call at the end of the sermon. I asked anyone who would dig in with me and not allow our church to die to come forward. There was not a dry eye in the place, and not one person remained in their seat. At the altar of that little church, we got on our knees. We were spiritually digging in. This was trench warfare, and we were not going to let Satan win.

We all prayed and cried and prayed again. It was a warrior's prayer. It was delivered out of the broken, desperate cries of our hearts and it moved the heart of God. That prayer in 1999 was the seed for the thousands and thousands of people that same church reaches now every single week.

From the battles fought in the fall of 1999, God has blessed our church with thousands of lives that have been changed by Jesus. What if we would have given up and given in? What if we would have retreated in the face of adversity, trials, tears, and difficulty? Do you need a miracle? We sure did. Most miracles happen so slowly you don't even know you're in the middle of one until you get to the other side. And I'm convinced I've been living a miracle since that day in 1999.

In the years since, the battles have been more intense. God uses one battle to prepare you for the next. I'm in yet another one even as I write the closing pages of this book. Hell's fury has been awakened once again. But whatever Satan means for evil, God is able to use for good. More than ever, I'm convinced the blessings received are more than worth the battles fought. In Romans 8:18, Paul tells us, *"For I consider that the sufferings of this present time are not worthy to be compared with the glory which shall be revealed in us."*

One day we will all gather before our Warrior King and inherit the Kingdom that is without end. We will reign forever with Him as priests and kings (Revelation 1:6, 5:10). The warfare will have been more than worth it. But until then, my prayer for you is that *"you may wage the good warfare"* (1 Timothy 1:18).

May *"the Lord bless you and keep you; the Lord make His face shine upon you, and be gracious to you; the Lord lift up His countenance upon you, and give you peace"* (Numbers 6:24-26).

ABOUT THE AUTHOR

Phil Hopper has been the Lead Pastor of Abundant Life Church in Lee's Summit, Missouri, since 2000. He watched God do extraordinary things in the life of the church as it has grown from 100 people to a megachurch touching thousands and thousands of people each week.

Prior to entering the ministry, he was a police officer and sergeant with the Kansas City Police Department where he served as a SWAT team member. It was through this experience that God uniquely prepared him for the ministry. Phil lives in the Lee's Summit area with his wife, Christa. They have three children: Jake, Makay, and Josh.